T0292628

Progress in IS

More information about this series at http://www.springer.com/series/10440

Stephan Kassel • Bing Wu
Editors

Software Engineering Education Going Agile

11th China–Europe International Symposium on Software Engineering Education (CEISEE 2015)

 Springer

Editors
Stephan Kassel
Westsächsische Hochschule Zwickau –
    University of Applied Sciences
Zwickau, Sachsen, Germany

Bing Wu
Dublin Institute of Technology
Dublin, Ireland

ISSN 2196-8705   ISSN 2196-8713   (electronic)
Progress in IS
ISBN 978-3-319-29165-9   ISBN 978-3-319-29166-6   (eBook)
DOI 10.1007/978-3-319-29166-6

Library of Congress Control Number: 2016940827

Printed on acid-free paper

This Springer imprint is published by Springer Nature
The registered company is Springer International Publishing AG Switzerland

The History of China-Europe International Symposium on Software Engineering Education

The China-Europe International Symposium on Software Engineering Education (CEISEE) was evolved from the China-Europe International Symposium on Software Industry-Oriented Education (CEISIE), which was founded in 2005, according to rapid development of software engineering education in both China and Europe.

The China-Europe International Symposium on Software Industry-Oriented Education was initialized from an international education project, EMERSION (Education to Meet the Requirements of Software Industry and Beyond—Establishing, Implementing and Evaluating an Industry-Oriented Education Model in China), supported by the "Asia-Link Programme" of European Commission, with the collaboration of the Dublin Institute of Technology (DIT) in Ireland and Harbin Institute of Technology (HIT) in China. During the EMERSION project, the project members shared the educational achievements and experience with more universities and institutes in Europe and in China.

In January 2005, the first China-Europe International Symposium on Software Industry-Oriented Education was held in HIT, Harbin, in China.

It was launched by the members of the EMERSION project, and the symposium's initial abbreviation was CEIS-SIOE. The second CIES-SIOE also took place in HIT, Harbin, in January 2006. At that conference, it was decided that the conference venue should alternate between China and Europe each year. So, in February 2007, the DIT in Dublin, Ireland, hosted the third China-Europe International Symposium on Software Industry-Oriented Education. Here, the initial abbreviation for the symposium was changed from CEIS-SIOE into CEISIE. January 2008 saw the fourth CEISIE symposium held at the Sun Yat-Sen University, Guangzhou, in China, and the fifth CEISIE symposium was at the University of Bordeaux 1 in Bordeaux, France, in May 2009. May 2010 saw the sixth CEISIE symposium taking place at the Northwestern Polytechnical University in Xi'an, China, while the seventh CEISIE symposium was hosted by the University of Northampton in Northampton in the UK.

It was then decided to change the name of the symposium from CEISIE into CEISEE (China-Europe International Symposium on Software Engineering Education), in order to extend the scope of the conference and to emphasize its focus on developing the discipline of software engineering. The eighth CEISEE symposium was at the Shanghai Jiaotong University in Shanghai, China, in May 2012, and the ninth CEISEE symposium was held by the University of Pavia in Milan, Italy, in May 2013. Last year, the tenth CEISEE symposium took place at the University of Electronic Science and Technology of China (UESTC), in Chengdu, China.

The CEISIE/CEISEE symposiums were very successful and attracted great attentions from educators, industrialists, and governmental officers, who are interested in software engineering education, across China and Europe. Until now, more than 650 participants from 16 countries, e.g., China, Ireland, UK, France, Germany, Italy, Spain, Switzerland, Sweden, Finland, Poland, Russia, USA, Australia, and South Korea, have attended symposiums.

The CEISEE aims at exploring new approaches to develop software engineering discipline and software engineering education in both China and Europe, according to the changing tendency of technical development of software engineering and educational requirements of the software talents all over the world. The CEISEE is a good platform for the educators, industrialists, and governmental officers related to software engineering education to exchange their ideas, to share their experience, and to develop their academic community in this domain.

CEISEE 2015: Topics

The 11th CEISEE symposium took place in Zwickau, Germany, in April 2015. It was organized by the Westsächsische Hochschule Zwickau – University of Applied Sciences. The theme of the CEISEE 2015 was *Going agile—bridging the gap between agility and budgets*. In general terms, the topics of CEISEE 2015 included:

- Education model for software engineering
- Innovation and evaluation of software engineering education
- Requirement and cultivation of high-quality software engineers for the future
- Curriculum for software engineering education
- Cultivating students to adapt to agile software engineering and customer requirements
- Software engineering for customizing information systems
- MOOC-based e-learning of software education
- Interdisciplinary education for budgeting IT projects

- Internationalization of software engineering education in globalization environment
- Quality assurance in software engineering education
- Cooperation model for industry and software engineering education
- Certification and authentication for professional education on software engineers

Zwickau, Germany   Stephan Kassel
Dublin, Ireland   Bing Wu

Contents

Contributors

David Chen IMS, University of Bordeaux, Talence Cedex, France

Dongming Chen Software College, Northeastern University, Shenyang, China

Yin Chen School of Software, Harbin Institute of Technology, Harbin, China

Dianhui Chu School of Computer Science and Technology, Harbin Institute of Technology, Harbin, China

Shengchun Deng School of Software, Harbin Institute of Technology, Harbin, China

Kaikun Dong School of Computer Science and Technology, Harbin Institute of Technology, Harbin, China

Wolfgang Golubski Westsächsische Hochschule Zwickau – University of Applied Sciences, Zwickau, Germany

Manja Görner Westsächsische Hochschule Zwickau – University of Applied Sciences, Zwickau, Germany

Frank Grimm Westsächsische Hochschule Zwickau – University of Applied Sciences, Zwickau, Germany

Yong Guo School of Software, Harbin Institute of Technology, Harbin, China

Gary J. Hill Computing and Immersive Technologies, University of Northampton, Northampton, UK

Lei Hong School of Information and Software Engineering, University of Electronic Science and Technology of China, Chengdu, Sichuan, China

Wen Jun-hao School of Software Engineering of Chongqing University, Chongqing, P.R. China

Stephan Kassel Westsächsische Hochschule Zwickau – University of Applied Sciences, Zwickau, Germany uthor_block">**Thomas Klein** Westsächsische Hochschule Zwickau – University of Applied Sciences, Zwickau, Germany

Dong Li School of Software, Harbin Institute of Technology, Harbin, China

Liu Ling School of Software Engineering of Chongqing University, Chongqing, P.R. China

Kaixu Liu Department of Industrial and Information Engineering, University of Pavia, Pavia, Italy

Tainy Ma Department of Industrial and Information Engineering, University of Pavia, Pavia, Italy

Sofia Meacham Software Systems Research Centre, Bournemouth University, Dorset, UK

Gao Min School of Software Engineering of Chongqing University, Chongqing, P.R. China

Gianmario Motta Department of Industrial and Information Engineering, University of Pavia, Pavia, Italy

André Pflüger SOPHIST GmbH, Nürnberg, Germany

Keith Phalp Software Systems Research Centre, Bournemouth University, Dorset, UK

Zhiguang Qin University of Electronic Science and Technology of China, Chengdu, China

Xiong Qing-yu School of Software Engineering of Chongqing University, Chongqing, P.R. China

Alexander Rauh Westsächsische Hochschule Zwickau – University of Applied Sciences, Zwickau, Germany

C.C.H. Rosen School of Computing and Mathematics, University of Derby, Derby, UK

Chris Rupp SOPHIST GmbH, Nürnberg, Germany

Tonghua Su School of Software, Harbin Institute of Technology, Harbin, China

Chengjie Sun School of Computer Science and Technology, Harbin Institute of Technology, Harbin, China

Zhiying Tu School of Software, Harbin Institute of Technology, Harbin, China

Scott Turner Department of Computing and Immersive Technologies, University of Northampton, Northampton, UK

Yan Wang IMS, University of Bordeaux, Talence Cedex, France

Xiaofei Xu School of Computer Science and Technology, Harbin Institute of Technology, Harbin, China

Lin Yao School of Software, Harbin Institute of Technology, Harbin, China

Xie Juan Wang Ye University of Electronic Science and Technology of China, UESTC, Chengdu, China

Zhang Yi School of Software Engineering of Chongqing University, Chongqing, P.R. China

Nan Yin Software College, Northeastern University, Shenyang, China

Linlin You Department of Industrial and Information Engineering, University of Pavia, Pavia, Italy

Ruiyun Yu Software College, Northeastern University, Shenyang, China

Dechen Zhan School of Computer Science and Technology, Harbin Institute of Technology, Harbin, China

Yan Zhao Zhang School of Information and Software Engineering, University of Electronic Science and Technology of China, Chengdu, Sichuan, China

Ting Zhong University of Electronic Science and Technology of China, Chengdu, China

Zhiliang Zhu Software College, Northeastern University, Shenyang, China

Reform and Practice of Laboratory Course for Compiler Principle in HIT

Yin Chen, Yong Guo, Lin Yao, Dong Li, and Shengchun Deng

1 Introduction

Compiler is a kind of important system software. Compiler principle is one of the professional and major courses in software engineering. The course is commonly regarded as one of the most difficult course with teaching and learn because of its difficult theory and abstract content [1, 3, 5]. Thus, laboratory is an important part of the course. Laboratory is a good way for students to master the relevant content and to stimulate students' interest. Due to the limited laboratory hours, we need to request students design the system in advance instead of work on it until laboratory class begins [2, 4]. Thus, there will be more discussion and evaluation time for students in class. This is a great improvement on laboratory course.

2 Brief Overview of the Laboratory Course

The "Compiler principles" course is offered in fall semester of the third college year, with total class time of 58 h (40 for lectures and 18 for laboratory). Three credits are given to this course and about 150 students attend the course each year.

(1) Laboratory contents and hours

The laboratory course includes three projects, namely design and implementation of lexical analyzer, design and implementation of syntax analyzer, and design and implementation of semantic analyzer. Each project takes two classes with 3 h for each class (see Table 1).

Y. Chen (✉) • Y. Guo • L. Yao • D. Li • S. Deng
School of Software, Harbin Institute of Technology, Harbin, China
e-mail: chenyin@hit.edu.cn; guo_yong@hit.edu.cn; yaolin@hit.edu.cn; lee@hit.edu.cn; dsc@hit.edu.cn

© Springer International Publishing Switzerland 2016
S. Kassel, B. Wu (eds.), *Software Engineering Education Going Agile*, Progress in IS, DOI 10.1007/978-3-319-29166-6_1

1

Table 1 Experiment contents and hours

No.	Project names	Hours
1	Design and implementation of lexical analyzer	3
2		3
3	Design and implementation of syntax analyzer	3
4		3
5	Design and implementation of semantic analyzer	3
6		3

(2) Laboratory assessment

The course assessment consists of two parts: operational skills (50 %) and experiment report (50 %).

(3) Equipment of laboratory teaching assistant

In the laboratory class, each teaching assistant (TA) will direct 15 students.

3 Problems of the Laboratory Course in the Past

(1) Insufficient preparation before laboratory class.

In the past, students almost did nothing before class. They usually began working on the project at the moment the lab class began. In fact, the laboratory task is rather heavy, even though having done much preparation, for many students, it is still considerably difficult to complete the programming task in several hours in class.

(2) Inadequate time for onsite check.

To guarantee quality of the laboratory, onsite check is a crucial link. It mainly includes program demonstration, checking of running result, explanation of source code etc. Checking for one student takes about 10 min. For 15 students, each TA will take about 150 min, which is just 3 teaching hours (50 min per teaching hour). Therefore, unless the TA(teaching assistant) starts checking the students' projects one by one since the beginning of the class, it is difficult to complete checking experimental results of all the students in class time. In fact, according to problem (1), many students cannot finish their projects in lab class, so they didn't get their work checked by TA. Without checking, we can't effectively evaluate students' work on the project. This is bound to affect quality of the laboratory.

(3) Ununiformed assessment standards among teaching assistants.

Sometimes, scores given by teaching assistants may be influenced by individual factors. Some teaching assistants may hold higher assessment standards and they tend to give higher scores, while others may hold lower assessment standard and they tend to give lower ones.

4 Reform and Practice of Laboratory Teaching

With regard to the problems listed above, we have taken some reform and practice methods as follows.

(1) Revised guideline of laboratory report.

In the past, students were only required, as preparation before experiment class, to understand the purpose and content of each experiment project. Such preparation is not enough for finishing the whole experiment smoothly. Now, we have revised the template of experiment report which now includes four parts:

- Project requirement analysis (10 points)
- Design of grammar (15 points)
- System design (15 points, including the outline design and detailed design),
- implementation of system and results analysis (10 points)

Among them, the first three parts are required to be finished before the first lab class of each project as preparation report (as mentioned above, each project takes two lab classes). Points will be deducted if these parts are not finished before the first class. In fact, from the viewpoint of software engineering, these are necessary analysis and design work to be finished before the formal performing on computer. The last part is permitted to be filled in after second class of each project.

The revised guideline of laboratory report involves various aspects of software implementation, and it reflects the cultivation of students' software engineering quality by this course.

(2) Ensure enough time for onsite check.

For many students, it is difficult to complete the experiment in class time of only several hours although they have taken much preparation, because of the heavy task. Therefore, students are encouraged to finish their project before the second (also the last) class of each project if they cannot ensure they can finish it in class time. Teaching assistant will onsite check students' work one by one at the beginning of the second class for each project so as to ensure adequate time to check all students' work of the group. If a student doesn't finished the project on time and not get checked by teaching assistant in class time, he will lose certain points. This is, in fact, a kind of inverted classroom, which requires students to learn and practice off class, and study, discuss and evaluate students' learning outcomes in class. Adequate preparation and practice before class can help students find more problems in advance and thereby ask their teaching assistant for help in the class. On the other hand, if they don't take adequate preparation and practice before class, it is rather difficult for them to find out the problems in the limited class time.

(3) Establish detailed evaluation criteria for operational skills.

Evaluation criteria for operational skills includes four parts:

- Finish the project on time and get it checked in class time (10 points)
- Correct running result (20 points)

Table 2 Detailed evaluation criteria for operational skills

Project name			Group number	TA name			
No.	Student ID	Student name	Scores of operational skills				
			Finish on time and get checked in class time (10)	Correct running result (20)	User-friendly interface, good demonstration (10)	Completeness of project documentation (10)	Total score (50)
1							
2							
. . .							
15							

- User-friendly interface, easy to operate, good demonstration effect (10 points)
- Necessary development notes or instructions in source program, complete application's documentation (10 points)

Every teaching assistant is required to fill in the following form in detail (Table 2).

(4) Organize training to teaching assistant.

We specially write a laboratory reference book for teaching assistants, which specifies laboratory contents, laboratory requirements, relevant theoretical knowledge and desired outcomes. We provide uniform training to teaching assistant based on this reference book and give detail explanation to some key points. On the other hand, in order to decrease the influence of individual factors in project evaluation, we need to balance the distribution of scores given by teaching assistants. So we require every teaching assistant to follow the principle that students with scores above 90 accounted for no more than 20 % in each group (3 persons), students with scores lower than 70 accounted for no less than 20 % in each group (3 persons).

(5) Share good works of former students.

Every year, we select some pieces of good works from former students and upload them onto the course website. It plays a very good role of guidance to current students. Practice has shown that the general level of current students' works got greatly enhanced.

5 Evaluation of the Proposed Methods

We'll evaluate the proposed methods in the following aspects.

(1) Proportion of students got projects checked in class

Table 3 shows number and proportion of students who got their projects checked in class. As can be seen that the proportions in 2012 are 77 %, 57 %

Table 3 Number/proportion of students got projects checked in class

Semester	Total number of students	Project 1		Project 2		Project 3	
		Number of students got checked in lab class	Proportion (%)	Number of students got checked in lab class	Proportion (%)	Number of students got checked in lab class	Proportion (%)
Fall 2012	139	107	77	79	57	45	32
Fall 2013	149	134	90	124	83	110	67
Fall 2014	144	140	97	125	87	111	77

and 32 % for project 1, 2 and 3 respectively. In 2013, the proportions are 90 %, 83 % and 67 %. In 2014, the proportions are 97 %, 87 % and 77 %. We began to implement this reform in 2013, so we can see, after this reform, most students got their work checked in class, and it surely help guarantee the quality of onsite check.

(2) Distribution of scores given by TA's

Figure 1 gives some data on distribution of scores given by TA's. For example, in 2012, for TA 1, 7 % of scores given by him falls in range 100 to 90, 40 % falls in range 90 to 80, and so on. So as TA 2 to TA 5. As can be seen from the figure that in 2012, the third TA gave more than 80 % of his scores to the range 90 to 80, so he tends to give higher scores. However, the first TA gave most of his scores to the range 80 to 70, so he tends to give lower scores. But after the reformation, in 2013 and 2014, TA's tend to give scores of similar distribution.

(3) Average scores of laboratory

Table 4 gives average scores of laboratory. As can be seen that average scores of 2012, 2013 and 2014 are 78.28, 80.09 and 82.98 respectively. Which shows that the general level of current students' works got greatly enhanced.

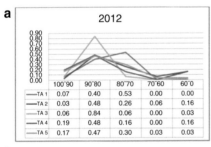

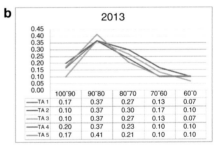

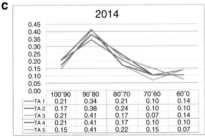

Fig. 1 Distribution of scores given by TA's

Table 4 Average scores of laboratory

Semester	Average score
Fall 2012	78.28
Fall 2013	80.09
Fall 2014	82.98

6 Conclusion

Laboratory is an important part of the course. According to the problems of laboratory course in the past, this paper talks about some improving methods, including revised guideline of laboratory report, ensure enough time for onsite check, establish uniformed assessment standards, share good works of former students. Practice has shown that with the reformed course, students get more passionate on compiler principle, and their ability of engineering practice is greatly enhanced.

References

1. Dongmei L, Haihu S.: Study and Exploration of the Teaching Methods for Course "Compiler Principle". Computer Education. 68, 103-104(2008)
2. Zongli J.: Teaching Design of the Course "Compiler Principle". Computer Education. 63, 26-30 (2008)
3. Man L.: Study on the Teaching Mode of Taking Students as the Center. China University Teaching, 2012(8): 32-36
4. Yuhui G.: Rational Thinking on the Teaching Reform of Principle of Compiler. Education and career, 2009(10): 84-85
5. Yu Z., Yiyun C., Qilong Z.: Research on Teaching Methods and Teaching Material Construction of the Course "Compiler Principle". China University Teaching, 2005(7): 61-62

A Philosophical Comparison of Chinese and European Models of Computer Science Education. (A Discussion Paper)

C.C.H. Rosen

1 Introduction

In May 2014, I was fortunate enough to be invited to a Chinese university to deliver a software development project management course to a mixed group of Chinese and European students on an international master's programme. The student cohort consisted of around 8 European students and 20 Chinese students and was taught over a 2 week period. The learning and teaching strategy consisted of a mixture of lectures, tutorial exercises, an investigation of a work related case study and guided reading typical of a European style master's programme.

This paper treats this experience as a case study presenting my observations, analysing and comparing the differing responses of the student groups and their acceptance of the teaching style. This is not a scientific or even a quasi-scientific study. There are far too few data points to make such a claim. Rather it is a personal interpretation. My aim is to postulate some general conclusions and stimulate discussion on the challenges faced in delivering a trans-cultural, industry oriented, software development programme and the cultural influences on higher education. I hope to avoid a doctrinal or judgemental account of my experiences. However, I am conscious of my own cultural influences and recognise how these might have biased my own thoughts. For this reason, I invite colleagues to contribute their own observations and consider how these might further the aims of CEISSE.

C.C.H. Rosen (✉)
School of Computing and Mathematics, University of Derby, Derby, UK
e-mail: c.rosen@derby.ac.uk

© Springer International Publishing Switzerland 2016
S. Kassel, B. Wu (eds.), *Software Engineering Education Going Agile*, Progress in IS, DOI 10.1007/978-3-319-29166-6_2

2 Learning and Teaching Philosophy

Before reporting and reflecting on my observations, I think that it is important to establish my learning and teaching objectives. This provides the basis and a benchmark against which any evaluation can be made. There is a clear danger in a study of this nature that the epistemological models of the observer lead to a self-reinforcing hermeneutic cycle that merely justifies the original epistemological model of the observer. Whilst I am conscious of this danger, it is one I cannot avoid other than by inviting criticism from peers. This I readily do.

The model of learning I ascribe to is represented in Fig. 1 below. This identifies three intersecting circles representing models of student learning which result in a highly industry oriented model of the purpose of higher education, although it could be used to position any learning and teaching strategy.

The three circles represent "content", "context" and "process". These circles intersect in a "Venn" style diagram because there are no clear boundaries between the three forms of knowledge. I do not wish to go into these in detail as this is not the purpose of this paper. The following paragraph therefore provides a brief overview of the model.

"Content" comprises of the theories pertinent to an academic domain, abstract knowledge associated with it and accumulated experience concerning the subject area. It is abstracted from any given situation. Content can normally be found in text books, journal papers etc. and is often delivered in HE settings through formal classes. Content is the domain that academia traditionally focused on delivering and, more particularly, developing, through on-going research.

"Context" is the application of a particular theory to a given context and requires practical/implementation skills. Vocational subjects generally give more emphasis in this sphere than the humanities, as, being able to deliver is an essential element of success. Context is situated in real world problems and encompasses knowledge and experience associated with practical problem solving. When employers

Fig. 1 Model of the learning process [1]

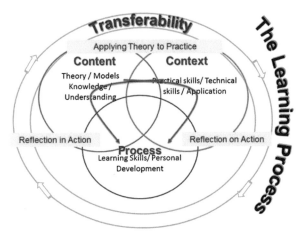

complain about the lack of readiness of graduates to work, it is often issues associated with this sphere that they complain about.

The association of context with competency contrasts with the association of content with understanding. An example of the difference between the two within the computing domain would be the capability of a student to program in a particular language (context) compared to an understanding of the principles of programming languages (content). In reality, both are needed. Students struggle to understand programming principles without knowing how to solve problems in a given language, yet they must understand the principles to be able to learn the range of languages they may be confronted with when they leave university. Most courses contain elements of both content and context. Examples and case studies are often used in teaching for just this purpose. Without context/application, abstract knowledge is interesting, but essentially unproductive.

An industry oriented approach to higher education is neither pure understanding nor technical excellence. It is the capability of transferring knowledge from one context to another. This requires the third sphere, "process".

Students need to develop their ability to learn independently, to use their knowledge and understanding to solve unfamiliar problems, to understand the processes and standards involved in learning and to recognise which tools and techniques are applicable to a particular context. In other words, students need the problem solving skills of logical reasoning, deduction, research and critical evaluation. These capabilities do not automatically emerge from content and context, but need to be nurtured and encouraged in equal measure through reflective practice.

In practice these components of the learning process overlap. This model suggests that learning activities contribute to the learning process by developing "reflection in action" and "reflection on action" [2].

My aim as a lecturer is to maximise students' recognition of the importance of process, even at the expense of content and context. This is in contrast to more traditional models of teaching which tend to prize content. This is not to devalue either content or context. Research, and hence new knowledge are situated in the content sphere and are clearly essential. Highly skilled practitioners, particularly reflective practitioners, feedback to theorists where models diverge from the real world. This points the way to further research. For me, in the institution I work in, developing the capabilities of observation, analysis and problem solving are core requirements for long term success in the knowledge economy. The learning and teaching style I adopt therefore (and this becomes particularly evident in the assessment methods) emphasises process. I expect students (particularly at Masters' level) to research content largely by themselves. Becoming skilled practitioners demands that they put in the practice hours. I can help with both of these, pointing the way to particular texts and suggesting alternative approaches to particular problems, but asking questions such as "why did you do that that way?" or "what alternatives did you consider?" encourages students to reflect on their own practice and develop meta-learning skills. To be consistent, assessment practice must reinforce this emphasis. The quality of the argument becomes more important than the content. Assessing this quality is problematic. This is the point at which academic cultures diverge. This can be identified by the level of student engagement in the process.

3 Student Engagement

Computing students tend to like solutions. Many like to be told the "right answer". If there are only optimised solutions and the critical questions are what to optimise and how, students tend to feel insecure. This appears to be true whatever their cultural background. Developing a sufficient sense of security to feel comfortable enough to challenge received wisdom is itself challenging. The established academic culture needs to support a process that encourages academic staff to support student transition from passive consumers of knowledge to active, self-motivated, independent learners. In the UK and across Europe demands for accountability have eroded this support, but it does nevertheless, still exist, at least in principle. My experience in China (and from discussions I have held with Chinese academics) suggests that this process is not as well understood. The objective of education authorities is to develop truly creative problem solvers, but they are unclear how the learning process and the learning and teaching approach required to achieve this outcome is inhibited by the existing academic culture.

The Chinese students I encountered (in general) were often confused by the demands I placed upon them in contrast to the European students who relished the opportunity to debate and argue. A few of the Chinese students did appreciate the chance to debate alternative and unorthodox perspectives, but the majority were more concerned to know what I believed so that they could give the "right" answer. The result was that, for this group of Chinese students, I found it difficult to engage them other than at a surface level. In the context of the course, this should not be considered surprising. The process required to facilitate student capability to engage and learn from this learning and teaching approach is extensive. Students need to develop confidence in the use of both intellectual and academic tools such as research skills, critical analysis and self-reflection to feel confident enough to challenge the authority of the teacher. And academic staff need to firstly provide the opportunity to allow students to engage in this way and also support them to do so by encouraging (and guiding) challenging responses.

Reference to the model illustrated in Fig. 1 may help to understand this phenomenon in more depth. I will refer to the UK education system as this is the one I know best, but this analysis may apply equally to most of Western and Northern Europe. Traditionally, British Secondary Education was split into two streams. One stream concentrated on knowledge acquisition (the content sphere) and was seen as a preparation for tertiary education. The other focused on practical skills (context) and minimised the demands of knowledge beyond the needs of the occupational domain. The objective of this education was utilitarian; providing sufficient resource for the economy. It was not designed to facilitate further study.

Tertiary education adopted a Socratic approach, building on the knowledge acquired at the secondary level to develop the link between content and process. Context was seen as lower status in the UK (less so in other European countries.) As the complexity of the work environment increased, the requirements of content in vocational education increased, but a binary divide still existed between the vocational stream and the academic stream until the demands of the knowledge economy outpaced the returns from a manufacturing economy. This led to a greater need to integrate all three spheres (content, context and process). As the UK did have a tradition of developing pure academic skill (process), and the interaction of context and content had already been established, it was not too difficult to graft on process skills to vocational (industry oriented) educational practice (although arguments continue over whether, and if so, how much process knowledge is required, and the status of this style of education remains lower than "pure" knowledge in the UK.)

The impression I have received is that in China, knowledge (content) is valued above other forms of academic attainment. This tradition is well established and inculcated into the education system. Both students and educationalists respect knowledge and find it difficult to accept that other forms of learning are at least as valuable if not more so. Questioning this perspective may be acceptable, but introducing the changes to support a different approach is more challenging. The assessment process needs to be consistent with the learning and teaching approach so provides a useful medium for observation and analysis.

Evidence supporting this observation regarding the significance of knowledge can be seen in the assessment regime. An assessment methodology that rewards knowledge over academic reasoning fails to support the Socratic process. It is easier, and there is less scope to discriminate between students, to test knowledge, but it is inconsistent with the objectives of developing the critical capabilities of students. Determining the academic capability of students on the grounds of the strength of the argument they present is much more subjective, and therefore a far less reliable instrument. This presents a dilemma for all academic administrations. In Europe it has led to discussion about the accountability of academic staff. How can management systems discriminate between good academic staff and those that fail to deliver? What constitutes a good member of academic staff? What are the assessment criteria? How do we improve our international standing if we cannot systematically identify poor performing staff?

My perception is that the connection between academic objectives and assessment policy is less well understood within the Chinese academic community than in Europe. For example, the use of multiple choice questions used on the course I taught on imply that there must be a correct answer. This form of assessment tests knowledge and the ability to recall that knowledge. Questions of this type cannot test a student's ability to use this knowledge or her/his understanding of the relative importance of it in different contexts. I would contend that an assessment method consistent with an industry oriented approach needs to test these latter skills rather than the former. To facilitate a transition from knowledge based learning to the development of critical evaluation skills, both the learning and teaching approach and the assessment methodology need to provide sufficient scope for the student to present their learning.

4   Conclusions

My experience of teaching in China last year has helped me to clarify my own objectives as a teacher. I have become more concerned with imparting to my students a regard for the learning process and the ability to reason with logic, based on valid evidence. I am less concerned to delivering content or even teach technical skills to them. As access to information becomes more widespread, quicker and more reliable, the need to deliver content diminishes. Much better, more professional and more eloquent resources exist at the touch of a button than I can hope to replicate. The need to understand this information, interrogate it and establish its value, escalates. Academic cultures, whether in Europe or in Asia, seem reluctant to accept the consequences of this technological change. An industry oriented approach must find ways of integrating content, context and process and of valuing each equally. In this paper I have not discussed how this might be achieved as this has been the subject of innumerable previous papers to this conference, including some of my own papers. This paper has sought, by comparing European and Chinese student response to my academic input, to identify some of the underlying difficulties inherent in the academic cultures we work in and to articulate how some of the preconceptions concerning academic value have arisen. I have presented an academic model which I hope helps to illuminate the academic process. Whilst European academic systems struggle to integrate content, context and process and have not recognised the constraints on accountability this results in, the Chinese system continues to value content in the expectation that this will of itself deliver innovation. Academics in both systems recognise the limitations resulting from the existing cultures, but seem more prepared to live with the contradictions than support the changes required to achieve innovative industry orientation. If this analysis is valid, then it presents those of us who wish to promote industry orientation with a dilemma. How do we reconcile genuine industry oriented approaches with the demands of prevailing academic processes? I would argue that the first step is to recognise that the dilemma exists, then to identify methodologies that might resolve the differences.

References

1. Rosen, C. C. H. and R. Schofield. Reliability and Validity in Work-Based Learning, 2011. Work Based Learning Futures V, Derby
2. Schön D. The Reflective Practitioner: How Professionals Think in Action, 1991 Aldershot, Arena.

Study of Progressive Training Plan on Software Engineering Talents

Zhang Yi, Wen Jun-hao, Liu Ling, Xiong Qing-yu, and Gao Min

1 Introduction

In order to meet Chinese strategic adjustment of economic structure and the development of software industry, the Ministry of Education approved the establishment of 35 national exemplary software schools in 2001. School of software engineering of Chongqing University is one of the national models. The national model of Software College boot from the undergraduate education, exploring on the software talents' training and the higher education system reform. These colleges are supposed to training a large quantity of multi-hierarchical, practical, with the international competitiveness of software engineering talents as soon as possible to meet the development of the Chinese software industry, and explore the possible way for Chinese higher education reform and innovation.

2 Software Engineering Talents Training Objectives and Program

2.1 Software Engineering Talents Training Objectives

In order to train qualified software engineers faster and better, a new type of software engineering talents' training system is the new problem we are facing. To do this, combined with the actual situation, through an in-depth study on software engineering talents cultivation pattern, the cultivating orientation—"relying on the local, the

Z. Yi (✉) • W. Jun-hao • L. Ling • X. Qing-yu • G. Min
School of Software Engineering of Chongqing University, Room 2-6 No. 11 Boshulin village, Section A, Shapingba District, Chongqing 400044, P.R. China
e-mail: cquzhangyi@cqu.edu.cn

© Springer International Publishing Switzerland 2016
S. Kassel, B. Wu (eds.), *Software Engineering Education Going Agile*, Progress in IS, DOI 10.1007/978-3-319-29166-6_3

west, facing the whole country, going-international" was put forward. By making reference to the experience of running colleges and universities at home and abroad, drawing lessons from the famous view of talents in IT companies, the "compound, application-oriented, internationalization" talents training goal was established. Accordingly, the software engineering talent training and course system based on progressive practice teaching system was drawn up.

2.2 Software Engineering Talents Program

In drawing up the program for software engineering talents training, through in-depth analysis of software engineering training program of the United States, Canada, India and other countries such as Ireland, consultation of a large number of domestic and foreign software talents training guiding documents, and repeatedly listening to Microsoft, IBM, as well as some software company as a reference. Software engineering talents' "the quality of knowledge and ability to structure" system was worked out, and as a basis for formulating a more scientific and reasonable talents training program and course system, as shown in Fig. 1.

The training program positioning in complex with technology and engineering, and the combination of software engineering and domain application, has clearly-defined hierarchy. The school of software engineering set the specialized courses around the development process of software engineering with new technology while emphasizing computer science and mathematics versus system engineering basis, to integrate the software technology with software engineering of new

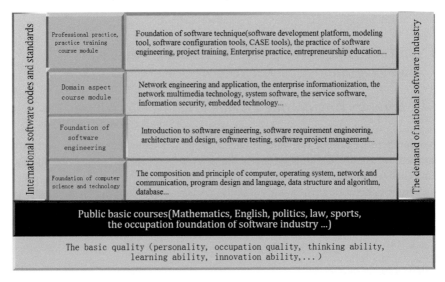

Fig. 1 The curriculum system of software engineering professionals

technology. The program emphasis on application-oriented features in software engineering field, and increase a large number of software projects practical courses to cultivate student ability to carry out software design independently.

In order to cultivate student's awareness of creativity and entrepreneurial capacity, the program must attach importance to practice teaching both inside and outside the classroom which play an irreplaceable role in training and developing student's ability and quality, at the same time enhancing the integration of course and extra-course practice teaching and make an overall program in the training program to form a complete practical teaching system. In practical teaching session, the program increasing the proportion of comprehensive and experiments design, which also strengthen the internship, project practices, courses design and the engineering training in part of graduate design to improve the student's innovation ability and practice ability throughout the training program.

3 Progressive Practice Teaching System of Software Engineering Talents

The ability of software development, analysis and solving problem is extremely important for software engineers. Through the development process of actual software projects improve software development and application skills.

Series courses based on progressive practice teaching system will guide students in learning software engineering knowledge, greater emphasize on cultivating the ability of practical application, improve students learning interest and enthusiasm, develop creative spirit, thus students are actively involved, instead of passively accept the classroom teaching. As a result, students can truly experience the whole process of software development.

3.1 Series Course Introduction Based on Progressive Practice Teaching System

The thought of training software engineering talents based on progressive practice teaching system has always been training throughout in software engineering professionals all aspects. And in the practical teaching, series courses arranged practice on software project, the training courses to cultivate students the actual engineering capabilities in software project as the goal, with modern software engineering theory and standardization of software process standards and regulations for the teaching of content framework. These series courses passed three stages of teaching and a total of three semesters to set up a series of objectives in teaching phase, which exercise student's practical engineering capabilities and cultivate the habit of normalization of software process gradually. These courses are important part of software engineering talents training system based on progressive practice teaching system.

3.2 Objectives of Series Courses Based on Progressive Practice Teaching System

The series courses established three phases of teaching goals.

The teaching objectives of the first phase are the ability of specifications for software construction. Specific sub-objectives:

1. Training students to have solid software encoding skills and cultivating the ability of analyzing and solving real programming problems.
2. Training students to have the standardization of software coding style, write out a commercial-level code quality software code and technical documentation for software code.
3. Training students to have collaborative development ability, familiar and master software construction and configure environment, use of CASE tools in the project and specification rational application.
4. Master the software unit testing techniques and methods.
5. Master the mainstream's newest software tectonic environment and platform.

The teaching objectives of the second phase are the ability of specification for software design and software testing. Specific sub-objectives:

1. Training students in software design and software testing, as a result, able to use commonly used design and test CASE tools and methods for software design and testing.
2. Training students in accordance with the idea of object-oriented to analyze actual engineering problems and make object-oriented model and reasonable to apply commonly used in the process of design patterns to solve practical design problems.
3. Training students of specifications for software testing, familiar with specifications and processes of software testing engineering.
4. Mastering commonly used testing tools and software testing methods in software project.
5. Training students to standardized software design and testing of technical documentation writing skills.

The teaching objectives of the third phase are standard software process and project management capability.

Specific sub-objectives:

1. In accordance with standardized software process standards training students to carry out software projects in order to standardize the software process standards as the guiding principle to organize the entire software lifecycle stages of the various sub–stages.

2. Familiar and master the skills of establishment and practical application for basic software process configuration environment, protect and improve the standard and efficiency of the project process by use the configuration management CASE tool.
3. Exercise of basic project management and risk control capabilities, able to use a certain method of project management and risk prevention measures to carry out the project team organization and risk control.

The teaching objectives of the above three stages are the training students specification of comprehensive software development capabilities goals step by step, the first phase of the teaching objectives and practices contents mainly including exercise capability of standardization engineering practice sub-procedure of software construction of software process, and the second phase focused primarily on software design and cultivate ability of standardization engineering practice sub-procedure of software testing, and the third phase have standardized software covers the entire process of the training project, as shown in Fig. 2.

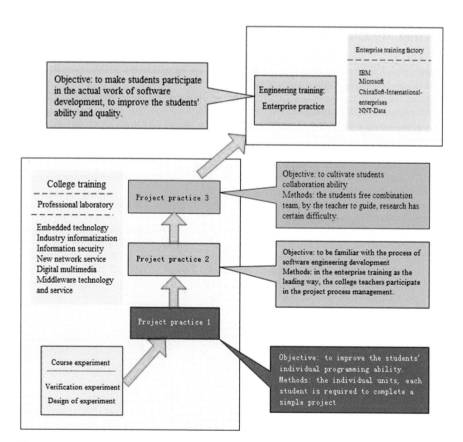

Fig. 2 Structure of the courses in progressive practice teaching system

4 Conclusions

School of Software Engineering, relying on local advantages, works out the software training program and course system based on progressive practice teaching system by actively exploring new approach to software engineering talents' cultivation in accordance with the education objectives. Through three stages of integrated courses on software project practice, the software training program and course system based on progressive practice teaching system can effectively compensate for the insufficient practice of university students and improve their adaptability and competitiveness to adapt to their future vocation more quickly. At the same time, we also recognize that there are still a number of problems on software talents training need to be further addressed, for example: continuous reform and deepening of teaching and talents' training; implementation and improvement issues of teaching quality assessment system, etc.

Acknowledgments Project support: The educating and training plan of Zhuo-Yue engineers

Further Reading

1. Wen Junhao. Research and practice of software engineering talent cultivation system. Research on Higher Engineering Education. 2005.4.
2. Zhang Yin, Yang Xiaohu, Chen Yue. "Software engineering" course in practice incentives for exploration. Computer education. 2007.5
3. Luo Bin, Zhang Liang, Shao Dong. Design of Course system of Software Engineering. China UniversityTeaching, 2005.1.
4. Wei Yingchun, Wen Jun-hao, Chen Shu-yu. Practice teaching system on the cultivation of the ability for school of software engineering. China higher education. 2011.2.
5. Li Yingmei, Huang Yu-yan, Xia Wei-ning, Exploration on applied software talents training of colleges and Universities. Education Exploration. 2011.6.
6. Tang Shukun, Li Jian. Manage model of soft engineering project in traditional industry. East China Economic Management. 2002.5
7. Chen Ying, Liang Yanming, Xiao Zexin. Based on the Value Engineering of Component Management in the Project Team Human Resource Allocation. Value Engineering. 2007.1
8. Li Hua, Luo Qiwu, Fu Chunyan. Practice of Improving Software Project Process Quality Based on Issue Management. Computer and modernization, 2007.4
9. Xu Ling, Wen Jun-hao, Xiong Qing-yu, Exploration and Practice of Training Mode for Software Engineering Talents. Computer education. 2010.6.

Agile Software Development in Business Informatics: Using Agile Methods for Teaching Purposes at the University of Applied Sciences, Zwickau

Manja Görner, Stephan Kassel, and Thomas Klein

1 Introduction

A growing number of software developers are using agile methods to code their products, aiming for increased productivity and a shorter time-to-market [1]. These practitioners demand a better teaching of agile methods in educational curricula of universities. They remark that the competencies of software engineers are often insufficient from their point of view [2].

Teaching basics of software engineering is also part of the information systems curriculum of business students at the Westsächsische Hochschule Zwickau – University of Applied Sciences in Zwickau, Germany (WHZ). Main part of the software engineering course is the proposition of a structured programming method like V model.

The government-funded research project EGNIAS resulted in the construction of a show room for a smart home environment. The show room is controlled by composite services, which are a collection of different controls for lighting, sound, etc. For instance, the user can choose a special lighting and low background music for dinner. This show room is an ideal application setting for teaching agile software development, thus making the learning situation quite attractive for the students.

In the following section, some agile methods are proposed, and some experiences of using them for teaching purposes are shortly presented. The goal lies in identifying suitable ones for integration into the curriculum of business students at WHZ.

M. Görner (✉) • S. Kassel • T. Klein
Westsächsische Hochschule Zwickau – University of Applied Sciences, PSF 201037, Zwickau 08012, Germany
e-mail: manja.franke@fh-zwickau.de; Stephan.Kassel@fh-zwickau.de; Thomas.Klein@fh-zwickau.de

© Springer International Publishing Switzerland 2016
S. Kassel, B. Wu (eds.), *Software Engineering Education Going Agile*, Progress in IS, DOI 10.1007/978-3-319-29166-6_4

2 Agile Software Development and Experiences in Teaching These Methods

In February 2001, seventeen proposers of Extreme Programming (XP), Scrum, Dynamic Systems Development Method (DSDM), Adaptive Software Development, Kristall, Feature-Driven Development (FDD), Pragmatic Programming and other methods met and proposed the necessity of an alternative to the document-centered approaches of heavy-weight software development processes. They published the Manifesto for Agile Software Development [3], in which they confessed

> **Individuals and interactions** *over processes and tools*
> **Working software** *over comprehensive documentation*
> **Customer collaboration** *over contract negotiation*
> **Responding to change** *over following a plan* [3]

Researchers embraced this manifesto, which is still valid [4], quite enthusiastically, and enhanced the methods afterwards [5, 6]. But the foundation of agile methods had already been laid in the 1990s, Scrum, eXtreme Programming (XP) and Feature-Driven Development (FDD) had been designed [7].

But the integration of these methods into software engineering curricula has been quite complex. Two approaches should be emphasized here to tackle the problems.

In the first approach, agile software development itself is the goal of teaching. Several scenarios have been developed, to practice different methods of agility and to experience their opportunities. One possible course program for beginners was proposed by Ramcke [8]. He involved the students into interactive games, whereby only some of the games included the development of software code. So the programming was not the main issue of this course, which had a weekly time of 180 min, adding up to 4 h workload per week. This had been perceived as a loss of time by the author. But RAMCKE also remarked, that part aspects of agile methods could be included in an activating teaching, which helps to integrate different software engineering methods.

Thurner [9] published her experiences of using agile methods for fundamental teaching purposes. She used a stepwise approach of teaching just the theoretical fundamentals which are needed for the next iterative increment of a software project. She concluded that students were happy with this iterative incremental teaching method. Students were better able to grasp connections between different topics. This is a very useful result especially in curricula where programming has a quite low priority, which is true for our teaching programs at the WHZ.

A second way to integrate agile methods into a curriculum lies in a practice course where agile methods have to be used. Nonnen et al. [10] have used a Kanban methodology for their university practice course. The focus of this course has been to introduce students to professional software development. The students already had some knowledge about agile methods like pair programming, or role playing. By using Kanban with a pull-principle and strictly limiting the individual phases of the project, the lecturers tried to encourage the students to solve that programming tasks which have been avoided in traditional programming as being boring or too complex. The Kanban board visualized the tasks and NONNEN observed that it was easier for the students to keep an overview of the overall task, leading to an explicit tackling of blocking tasks, and resulting in better student projects.

3 Concept for the Use of Agile Methods Within the Business Computer Science at the WHZ

3.1 The Fundamental Approach

Over the past year the project EGNIAS was accomplished at the WHZ. In this connection, a model of a smart home was created in the form of a pattern room. Therefore a room control system was designed which includes so called composite services. According to his or her planned activities, the user selects a composite service whereupon the room adjusts to these activities by providing the right atmosphere. Therefore energy consumers are specifically switched on or off so that lighting scenarios and as well as quiet background music are offered while eating.

With the aim of increasing compatibility with other systems in the home automation system these composite services were mapped by using an ontology which was designed for this purpose particularly.

The pattern room is now available for teaching.

3.2 The Pattern Room

This experimental model "pattern room" has an internal dimension of approximately $140 \times 90 \times 50$ cm (W $\times$ D $\times$ H). The room is divided into an entrance area, a working area, a dining area, a lounge area and a reading area (Fig. 1). Six power outlets and four dimmable LED lamps were installed in the room. Furthermore a floor lamp is installed and connected to a specific electrical outlet.

Technically, the room control is realised by a PLC. The user accesses the room's control via the control panel next to the door or by using a tablet based interface. Here, the user can choose between different services (eating, working, reading, . . .). Depending on the user's planned activity he or she selects a service (composite service), whereby the room control sets itself on this scenario. For example a corresponding light scenario.

The creating of such control systems should be the main content of the designed course.

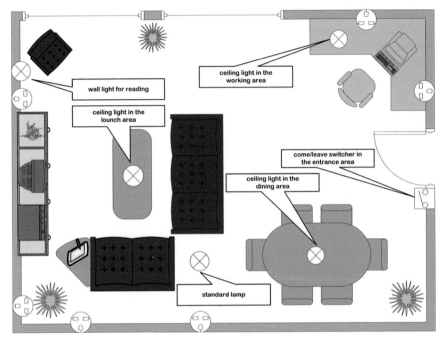

Fig. 1 Pattern room

3.3 Classification in the Study Process and Desired Development of Skills

For students of Industrial and Business Management as well as Business Administration, the course Business Computer Sciences is provided in the first and second semesters. In the first semester a lecture with a volume of 60 contact hours and an exercise with 30 contact hours will be held. In the second semester lecture and also exercise include each two contact hours. During the course basic economics computer sciences as well as aspects of the Operations Research and System Management are taught.

The systems of the modern world are shaped by processes of information processing. Therefore, students have to be enabled to understand, to plan, design and apply information systems and the immanent processes interdisciplinary and efficiently. The aim for the students of a university is to develop the necessary understanding, to acquire the relevant knowledge and stamp out basic skills of practical use. Experience has shown that students indeed are able to understand the design of a process principle (input, throughput, output), but they have difficulties in applying this concept practically, especially if it is an unusual topic for them. Therefore students should train their ability to analyze unknown processes and to develop new processes.

Because of working in practice with different information systems, the students are supposed to learn what is to do in order to work with systems which include different semantics. For this purpose students should learn the terms semantics and semantic networks. They should find out what different semantics within a control system are in action. First, the components and consumers are to be regarded as hardware. They are interconnected by standards. Secondly, they have to understand the control software perspective. Here the concept of the mentioned composite services is implemented. A third aspect represents the different users. It is to analyze what users actually want—what do they expect from their smart home—and how does the room react in contrast. For example it is important to note, that a person perceives a specific light intensity differently in varying situations.

3.4 Possible Use of the Pattern Room in Teaching

It is assumed that the students participating in the course have no experience in PLC programming. So it is necessary to learn the programming language. This should be in focus of the teaching activity. Therefore, students should be given the appropriate available manual.

The programming techniques could be taught by Thurner's method. This would have the advantage that the students recognize immediately the effect of the techniques and do not feel overwhelmed. The following incremental program elements could be worked out:

Step 1: Control of a single lamp without any dimming
Step 2: Control of a single lamp with dimming
Step 3: Programming of two services (one lamp with full power, the other one off; one lamp with half power and the other with full power)
Step 4: Programming a lamp control, which takes external light contamination into account (incorporation of brightness sensors)

Now the students are familiar with the most important techniques and are ready to create the room control independently. The agile software development methods can be used. It is always particularly important to help the students to keep track of the whole project. A Kanban board is an appropriate instrument for this task. It is advisable to divide the overall program into several small teams. To organize these teams and to manage individual programming tasks, the methods Scrum or FDD are suitable. XP provides a suitable distribution of roles. The instructor takes at the same time the role of the customer and the expert. In the presence of two carers, the roles can be separately assigned in accordance. The method of pair programming will allow students to derive mutual benefit from the capabilities of the partner. During compiling the teams should take care that better students get together with those who cope less well with software development. By this division the teams can be set up so that they are equal productive and each team contributes an equal share

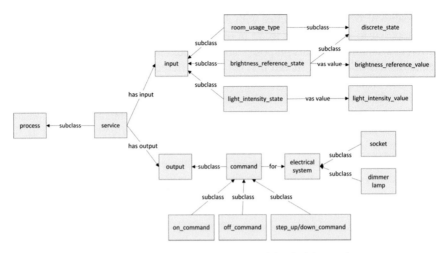

Fig. 2 Illustration of composite services in the conceptual level of the ontology

to create the control. This circumstance will strengthen the team spirit of the whole group.

The coach in the role of the customer should create the task accordingly the following steps. At first he or she communicates a rough idea of the control, then he or she refines and varies his or her requirements step by step, according to a customer who changes his or her requests during the program creation. In addition to the learning PLC programming, students can become familiar with the topic "semantic networks and ontologies". In the project EGNIAS designed composite services (Fig. 2) were represented in an ontology. After the introduction of the topic and this particular ontology, program parts could be provided to the students. Now they must decide if this is a program part of a composite service. If this is confirmed, this additional service has to be integrated in the room control. Through out these lessons the student should be able to recognize the contribution of ontologies for interoperability.

4   Conclusion

The application of the pattern room in teaching provides students with the opportunity to develop different skills. By applying agile methods of software development, they can define their own focus and yet must simultaneously manage the complexity of the system. System boundaries have to be defined autonomously in order to reduce the complexity. This is done individually, so that depending on student's ability the complexity is detectable. Then more and more aspects can be brought in. The complexity increases gradually, this happens controlled. At the same time students get the exponential growth of complexity shown. This gives them an understanding of the complexity of real systems they are working with. Also the practice of soft skills will be trained. The students have to complement each other in their professional skills and team communication plays an essential role. The handling of a customer can also be practiced, which is a respectable capacity especially in field of business administration. Overall, the use of the pattern room and the application of agile methods in software development in the teaching offers many opportunities to enhance teaching quality and increases its attractiveness in the eyes of students.

References

1. Version One: State of Agile. 8th annual survey. http://www.versionone.com/pdf/2013-state-of-agile-survey.pdf (3.12.2014)
2. Martin Kropp, Andreas Meier: Swiss Agile Study 2012. Agile Software-Entwicklung in der Schweiz. Fachhochschule Nordwestschweiz. Zürcher Hochschule für Angewandte Wissenschaften. http://www.swissagilestudy.ch/docs/SwissAgileStudy2012.pdf (3.12.2014)
3. http://agilemanifesto.org/ (3.12.2014)
4. Michelle Bowles Jackson: Agile: A decade in. In: PM Network. April 2012. S. 60-62.
5. Tore Dyba, Torgeir Dingsøyr: Empirical studies of agile software development: A systematic review. In: Information and Software Technology 50 (2008) S. 833–859.Torgeir Dingsøyra
6. Sridhar Nerurc, VenuGopal Balijepally und Nils Brede Moea: A decade of agile methodologies: Towards explaining agile software development. In: The Journal of Systems and Software 85 (2012) S. 1213– 1221.
7. Petri Kettunen: Adopting key lessons from agile manufacturing to agile software product development—A comparative study. In: Technovation 29 (2009) S. 408–422.
8. Eike-Christian Ramcke: Kompetenzaufbau für die agile Softwareentwicklung mit Hilfe eines didaktischen Methodenbaukastens zur Entwicklung individueller Lehrkonzepte. Bachelorarbeit. Hochschule für Angewandte Wissenschaften Hamburg. Eingereicht am 23.11.2014.
9. Veronika Thurner: Iterativ-inkrementelle Vermittlung von Software-Engineering-Wissen. In: A. Spiller, H. Lichter (Hrsg.): Softwareengineering im Unterricht der Hochschulen. 13. Workshop. Tagungsband. S. 71-78.
10. Jan Nonnen, Paul Imhoff, Daniel Speicher: Kanban im Universitätspraktikum. Ein Erfahrungsbericht. In: A. Spiller, H. Lichter (Hrsg.): Softwareengineering im Unterricht der Hochschulen. 13. Workshop. Tagungsband. S. 91-98.

© DOI 10.1007/978-3-319-29165-9

International Program Strategy for Software Engineering Skills Development in Software College at NEU

Dongming Chen, Ruiyun Yu, Nan Yin, and Zhiliang Zhu

1 Introduction to NEU and Its Software College

Northeastern University (NEU) was established in 1923, located in Shenyang, Liaoning Province. It is one of China's most preeminent universities and is designated as one of the national key schools, as part of China's national "211 Project" and "985 Project". Founded on September 28, 2002, Software College (SC) of NEU is one of the 35 pilot software colleges first approved by the Chinese Ministry of Education. Our Software College focuses on "training practical, interdisciplinary and international professionals with the spirit of time and pioneering, who can meet the demands of social development and new international trends" [1, 2].

We cooperated closely with companies at home and abroad and have established joint laboratories with IBM and Neusoft amongst others. Off-campus practice bases have been founded in more than 20 companies, including IBM, Alibaba, Tmall, Baidu, etc. The Software College has also promoted close ties internationally with foreign universities. Today, Internationalization is widely accepted, software college of NEU also cooperates with a number of foreign universities and educational institutions [3, 4]. After 12 years operation, the college has obtained rapid development in many aspects and became a competitive and influential group in software talents cultivation [5].

D. Chen (✉) • R. Yu • N. Yin • Z. Zhu
Software College, Northeastern University, Shenyang, China
e-mail: chendm@mail.neu.edu.cn

© Springer International Publishing Switzerland 2016
S. Kassel, B. Wu (eds.), *Software Engineering Education Going Agile*, Progress in IS, DOI 10.1007/978-3-319-29166-6_5

2   The Main Characteristics of the Education Insights

We advocate cooperation with industries, cooperation with foreign universities and institutes, running college with various models [6, 7]. The following denotes the fundamental ideology:

1) Being guided by the demands of industry makes our approach more practical;
2) Combining with the specific domains other than software engineering trains students the ability of solving interdisciplinary problem;
3) Facing the world brings us international vision.

We carry out '611 mode' for undergraduates, that is, among the 4 years of undergraduate study, there are six semesters' course learning, one semester's technical training and one semester's thesis (final project). This ensures the students to strengthen project development capability and experience before employment, thus enhancing their competitiveness.

3   Degree Programs in Software College of NEU

3.1   Bachelor Programs for Software Engineering

We seek to provide students with theoretical fundamentals of software development coupled with an appreciation and understanding of practical aspects and competencies required by industry [8, 9]. The program is designed to foster innovation through flexibility of software engineering as a business problem-solving discipline. Students in this level take these core courses: advanced mathematics, advanced algebra, basic electronic technology, discrete mathematics, C language, C++ program design, data structure, principle of computer composition, database systems, computer network, software engineering, software testing technology, software requirement analysis and design, software architecture and design patterns.

3.1.1   International Class (English) of Software Engineering

(1) **Basic situation of the class**

1. A special class which has its own training program.
2. Strengthen English abilities of the students. Students are required to pass CET4 in the first semester, pass CET6 in the second semester, and communicate freely with foreign teachers from second year.
3. 90 % of compulsory professional courses are given by foreign teachers.
4. Students may have more opportunities to study aboard.

5. Students are supposed to become the talents with a solid capability of English and professional skills.

(2) **Graduates of Grade 2010 in International class (English) of Software Engineering**

In total, there are 34 graduates in this class, and each of them achieved a good destination after graduation, which shows the success of the special class. Seventeen students went abroad for further study. Four students were admitted to Carnegie Mellon University, US; One student was admitted to Sydney University; 1 student was admitted to Imperial College, UK; 1 was admitted to Hong Kong City University; 3 students joined the cooperative programs of SC in Loughborough University, UK, Missouri University, US and Dublin City University, Ireland. It is worth mentioning that one student was admitted by 8 famous world-wide universities including Columbia University, University of Pennsylvania, Carnegie Mellon University, US Northeastern University, etc. Four students went on study in China: they were admitted to Peking University, Zhejiang University, University of Science and Technology of China and Northeastern University. Thirteen students started work in related industries: they were employed by famous IT & software companies such as Baidu, Netease, Sohu, Ctrip, Neusoft, etc.

3.1.2 International Class (Japanese) of Software Engineering

The location of NEU is not far from Japan, there are large skills demands for Japanese industry and some students would rather go to work in Japan or Japanese company in China. In order to adapt to this condition, we established another special class of the software engineering major. We positioned the class as follows: (1) Strengthen both Japanese and English abilities of the students. Students are required to pass CET4 in the first academic year, pass N2 in the second year, and communicate freely with Japanese teachers from third year. (2) Students may have more opportunities to study aboard, especially Japan. (3) Students are developed into skilled graduates with a solid capability of Japanese skill, English skill and professional skills, and then are turned into more competitive. Up to now, about 30 graduated students of our college went to work in Japan, and these students enlarged the cooperation between our college and Japanese companies/industries.

3.1.3 Software Engineering (English Program)

At present, 5 undergraduate students enrolled in software engineering of NEU and most of them came from the third world, we still hope to expand the scale and attract more students from European and American countries. We are looking forward to establishing an independent class for international students in the near future. The English program for Bachelor has the following characteristics:

1) Academic period: 4 years.
2) All courses are given in English, except Chinese Language.
3) 95 % of compulsory professional courses are given by foreign teachers.
4) Foreign teachers are the professors or lecturers from UK, USA, Ireland, etc.
5) More than 3 months internship in famous IT companies in the sixth semester.

3.2   Master Programs for Software Engineering

We aim at making students to be software engineering leaders. The program teaches students to apply computer science, engineering, and mathematical principles to design, develop, and test software. The core of the program is centered on learning to make professional judgments by honing essential critical thinking skills.

For master programs, we set up two types of degrees—academic degree and professional degree, according to the demand of ministry of education. Based on the domain of software engineering and research foundation of professors in our college, we focused on the following research areas: for students of Academic Degree, we provide "Complex system theory and application technology, Multimedia application technology, Big data computing and applications, Network and information security, Trusted software technologies, Virtual reality and simulation technology", and for students of Professional Degree, "Software services and applications, Mobile Internet technology and applications, Clouding computing and applications, Game and animation technology, Information system security and applications, Chaos & fractal technology and applications, Complex network technology and applications" are offered.

3.2.1   Software Engineering (Chinese Program)

The courses for Chinese program are taught in Chinese or bilingually (Chinese-English). It started from 2010 and we have more than 60 students per year, and the majority of them are professional degree [10].

For professional degree, we follow the framework of "Excellent Software Engineers Plan" of MOE of China, emphasize practical training, and send students to industry to participate real project research and development for at least 6 months [11].

3.2.2   Software Engineering (English Program)

The courses for English Program are taught in English. It is suitable for international students with relatively good English from other countries to China. Nine foreign students are enrolled in 2013, 12 students in 2014, and the program is running well.

In the second year, we sent these students to Neusoft—the biggest software company in China for practical training. These students sang high praise for the excellent environment and solid real project training. We will continue to consolidate the university-industry cooperation mechanism. Features of the English Program are shown below:

1) Academic period: 2.5 years (1 year—course learning, 0.5 year—internship, 1 year—thesis)
2) English Taught Program: All courses (except Chinese language and Chinese culture) are given in English.
3) Collaborate with International IT Enterprises: Through in-depth cooperation between Software College and Neusoft, the students who join in the graduate program will stay in Neusoft at least half a year in order to experience professional courses, project training and internship [12, 13].

3.3 Ph.D. Program for Software Engineering

The education objectives of Ph.D. program for software engineering are as follows: Mastery of a solid rudimentary knowledge and systematic professional knowledge in the discipline of software engineering; understand the cutting-edge research in the discipline and obtain the ability to carry out relevant research. Students should have some original research achievements; possess the ability of undertaking scientific research or the ability to take on the work of engineering technology; can skillfully read foreign materials in this discipline and have a command of foreign language speaking and writing skills as well. The research areas for Ph.D. program include: software services and applications, system complexity and applications, multimedia applications, trusted software technology, key technologies for E-commerce security, service computing, Web information processing, self-adaptive software theory and technology, reliable netware theory and technology, cloud computing and complex network applications. At present, we have two international Ph.D. students.

3.4 Achievements of International Education

Figure 1 shows the rate of going abroad of grade 2008–2010 (graduated from 2012 to 2014) undergraduate students in three majors (Information Security and Digital Media Technology are the other two majors in Software College of NEU, but software engineering holds about 70 % of students). From Fig. 1, we can see that about 20 % software engineering undergraduate students had overseas experiences or went abroad after graduation in 2014.

Figure 2 gives the number of undergraduate students going abroad for exchange and for further study after graduation in the recent 5 years.

Fig. 1 The rate of students going abroad in the latest 3 years

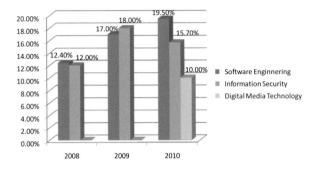

Fig. 2 The number of students going abroad in recent 5 years

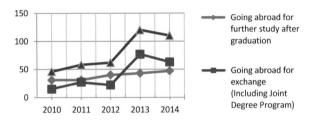

4 International Cooperation of Software College of NEU

After 10 years, especially the latest 5 years, we cooperated with some Partner Universities from US, Australia, Japan, UK, Ireland, Canada, France and Italy.

At the same time, we enhanced the cooperation with Partner Enterprises, such as Microsoft, IBM, Oracle, Google, HP, Baidu, Hitach, NEUSOFT, etc.

By far, we set up multiple joint programs for both undergraduates and Masters, which are detailed below.

(1) **Double Bachelor Degree Programs**

    1) 2 + 2 Double Bachelor Degrees Program, SWCNEU and Monash Univ., Australia

    2) 2 + 2 Double Bachelor Degrees Program, SWCNEU and Univ. of Missouri Columbia, US

    3) 2 + 2 Double Bachelor Degrees Program, SWCNEU and the Univ. of Colorado in Boulder, US

    4) 3 + 1.5 Double Bachelor Degrees Program, SWCNEU and Univ. of Wollongong, Australia

(2) **Bachelor and Master Degree Programs**

    5) 3 + 1 + 1 Bachelor and Master Degrees Program, SWCNEU and Loughborough Univ., UK

    6) 3.5 + 1.5 Bachelor and Master Degrees Program, SWCNEU and Aberystwyth Univ., UK

7) 3.5 + 1.5 Bachelor and Master Degrees Program, SWCNEU and Dublin City Univ., Ireland

8) 3 + 2 Bachelor and Master Degrees Program, SWCNEU and Univ. of Missouri Columbia, US

9) 3 + 2 Bachelor and Master Degrees Program, SWCNEU and Missouri Univ. of S&T, US

10) 3 + 1 + 2 Bachelor and Master Degrees Program, SWCNEU and Valenciennes Univ., France

11) 4 + 1 + 2 Bachelor and Master Degrees Program, SWCNEU and Valenciennes Univ., France

(3) **Double Master Degree Programs**

12) 1 + 1 + 0.5 Double Master Degrees Program, SWCNEU and Hosei Univ., Japan

13) 1 + 1 + 0.5 Double Master Degrees Program, SWCNEU and Pavia Univ., Italy

(4) **Short-term Student Exchange Programs (2–4 weeks)**

14) Loughborough Univ., UK Summer School

15) Univ. of Utah, US Winter/ Summer Study Tour

16) Ritsumeikan Univ., Japan Exchange Program

We had also cooperative programs in NEU for Chinese student exchange (1–2 semesters), with 32 universities from 12 countries/areas. In order to support the international talents cultivation, we employed foreign teachers to give full English courses for our students. Up to now, totally 32 courses were conducted by foreign teachers in our college.

5 Conclusions

This paper introduces the features of software engineering skills and abilities development of Software College at NEU and the related international works are mainly discussed. Software College of NEU took solid steps on the road of the international talents cultivation and we are looking forward domestic and foreign counterparts to carrying out extensive cooperation and communication. We deeply believe that through our joint efforts, the paces of international talents cultivation of software engineering specialty would be accelerated, the cooperation and communication would be constantly deepen, the talents cultivation quality would be remarkably improved.

Acknowledgements The paper is partly supported by Project of graduate education funding of Northeastern University: Research and exploration of Innovative learning for graduates (2013), the education and science of the "12th Five-Year Plan" project of Liaoning province: Study on individual talents cultivation mode based on education big data (2014), project of curriculum system construction for academic degree graduates from Ministry of Education of China: curriculum of software engineering for software college at NEU (2015).

References

1. Chengming Li, Lei Zhang, Xiaoyang Wang. Thinking of international talents training, CHINA HIGHER EDUCATION, 2013.6, 18-20, 36.
2. Jiaqiang Tao, Shigao Chen. Study on international talents cultivating mode for university, The Guide of Science & Education, 2014.12, 12-13.
3. Zhuo Wang. Exploration and practice on cultivating mode for international practical software talents, XueYuan, 2013(17), 21-22.
4. Tao Tan, Yaming Wang, Xuemei Li. Exploration and Practice of International Software Talents Cultivation, Computer Education, 2010.5, 9, 13-16.
5. Dongming Chen, Zhiliang Zhu and Dongqi Wang. Rethinking the talents cultivation mode of software engineering, Software Engineering Education for a Global E-Service Economy, Progress in IS, Springer International Publishing Switzerland 2014, 2014.1, 93-100.
6. Wei Lu, Yuanyuan Cai, Weiwei Xing. Reform and innovation of the international software personal training mode, Research in Higher Education of Engineering. 2013(1), 76-83.
7. Ling Xu, JunHao Wen, Yu Xiongqing. Exploration and Practice of Training Mode for Software Engineering Talents, Modern Educational Technology, 2013, 23(8), 118-121.
8. Nan Yin, Ruiyun Yu, Zhiliang Zhu. Exploration on international talents cultivation for software engineering, computer education, 2014.9, 11.
9. Hujie Huang, Peijun Ma. Practice on education system for international and industrial master of software engineering, computer education, 2015(1), 7-9, 13.
10. Dongming Chen, Yi Ma. Teaching research on innovative learning for graduates, computer education, 2014.9, 17, 84-87.
11. Yonghui Ma, Yang Shi. Research on cultivation mode of international talents based on school-enterprise cooperation, Heilongjiang Researches on Higher Education, 2013(2), 148-150.
12. Qichun Huang, Hongguang Fang. Research on the Quality Assurance System of Software Engineering Education, 2013 International Conference on Education and Teaching, 446-451.
13. Hongjiang Pang, Huan Chen. New thinking of graduates training for software engineering professional degree, education exploration, 2013(10), 54-55.

Outstanding Engineer Education Plan for School of Information and Software Engineering at UESTC

Ting Zhong and Zhiguang Qin

1 Introduction

School of Information and Software Engineering (SISE) at University of Electronic Science and Technology of China (UESTC) was founded in 2001 and is the first batch of 35 demonstrative software schools in China. SISE of UESTC was originally called School of Software Engineering. The name was changed to School of Information and Software Engineering with also the change of whole education plan in 2011. Before 2011, the education plan of SISE had no much difference from the education plan of other schools of UESTC. For the grades before grade 2012, for the first 7 semesters, students of SISE stay on campus for course study. In the last semester, students of SISE do a project and finish their undergraduate thesis under the guidance of SISE teachers. Starting from grade 2012, education plan of SISE put more focus on cooperating with enterprises. Since then, students are expected to spend at least 1 year at companies for engineering training. The objective of the education plan is to cultivate outstanding engineers. So the new education plan is called Outstanding Engineer Education Plan. After almost 4 years' practice of Outstanding Engineer Education Plan, there are both achievements and problems.

In this paper, we will first talk about the plan itself. Then the quality assurance measures, the problems and the countermeasures will be discussed.

T. Zhong (✉) • Z. Qin
University of Electronic Science and Technology of China, Chengdu, China
e-mail: zhongting@uestc.edu.cn

© Springer International Publishing Switzerland 2016
S. Kassel, B. Wu (eds.), *Software Engineering Education Going Agile*, Progress in IS, DOI 10.1007/978-3-319-29166-6_6

37

2   Schedule of Outstanding Engineer Education Plan

SISE has Software Engineering as a national characteristic major for undergraduates. This major consists of eight directions: Software Technology, Embedded Systems, Mainframe, Network Security Engineering, Information Engineering, Information Acquisition and Control, Computer-aided Design and Engineering, Digital Animation. So the curriculums are diversified. Although every direction has different syllabus, they shared similar teaching schedule. Table 1 shows the detailed schedule for Outstanding Engineer Education Plan.

Illustrations for Table 1:

1. All content listed in Table 1 is mandatory. To encourage students to cultivate International vision, with necessary application process, the Enterprise Internship can be substituted by study abroad program.
2. For Summer Holiday Internship, students are usually sent to technology training organization and companies. The training fee is paid by SISE. A lead teacher is assigned to every student group for safety supervision and training process control.
3. For Course Experiments, students are divided into small group. They are guided by SISE teachers to finish a small project on campus.
4. For Modern Information Engineering Enterprise Practice, through the way of two-way choice, students are sent to companies for internship. Companies will provide training, accommodation, necessary resources and sometime nominal salaries for SISE students. Every student is required to participate in a project at a company and submit weekly reports and a project summary to a SISE teacher.

Table 1 Schedule of Outstanding Engineer Education Plan with respect to company internship

Contents	Duration
Semester 1 and semester 2	
Visit to the local IT companies	2 days
Summer holiday after semester 4	
Summer holiday internship	4 weeks
Semester 5	
Course Experiment I	32 class hours
Enterprise Cooperation Course I	16 class hours
Semester 6	
Enterprise Cooperation Course II	16 class hours
Enterprise Cooperation Course III	16 class hours
Modern Information Engineering Enterprise Practice I	4–8 weeks
Course Experiment II	32 class hours
Semester 7	
Modern Information Engineering Enterprise Practice II	16 weeks
Semester 8	
Undergraduate Thesis	16 weeks

5. For Semester 8, students are required to write an undergraduate thesis at a company. Different from Modern Information Engineering Enterprise Practice, this stage put more emphasis on the writing of thesis.
6. Enterprise Cooperation Courses are very flexible courses in which course contents can be about any knowledge in software engineering. Not like regular courses at SISE which usually last a semester or half a semester, Enterprise Cooperation Courses can be taught in a compact style. For the convenience of enterprise course teachers, Enterprise Cooperation Courses are arranged on weekends or at nights.

3 Quality Assurance Measures

3.1 School Council Accountability System

School Council is organized to control the internship process and the training quality. School Council takes the role of supervision and evaluation. For example, School Council is responsible for evaluating qualification of companies and Enterprise Cooperation Courses teachers.

3.2 Strict Company Qualification Examination and Process Controls

SISE only works with well-known companies whose assets and reputation meet certain requirements. Interested companies should first submit qualification documents such as photocopy of its business license to SISE together with application forms. In application forms, companies must provide detailed descriptions of their internship programs with the following information: the number of students they will recruit for each project, description of objectives and contents of the projects, description of minimum requirements on students' skills or prerequisite course list and the final training objectives. Those qualification documents and application forms will be discussed by School Council. Workload, degree of difficulty, feasibility and values of training will be well assessed by School Council before the company being qualified to be selected by students. SISE will then send descriptions of projects to all students and arrange two-way choice interview between companies and students. After that, companies will sign tripartite agreements with SISE and the students that they accepted. In those agreements, the responsibilities of the companies for students' safety, the training objectives, the salaries and the resources allocated for the internship are described.

3.3   Enterprise Cooperation Course Selection

The teachers for Enterprise Cooperation Courses are recommended by cooperative companies. They must have at least 5 years' practical experience in research and development at enterprises and have advanced technical job title granted by Chinese government.

3.4   Responsibilities of SISE Teachers for Internship

For Summer Holiday Internship, SISE will send a lead teacher to supervise the whole internship process at the training site. Lead teachers are required to supervise the students' safety and attendance time. They should also communicate with companies so that companies can better adapt their courses and projects to the needs and the abilities of most students. They are required to report daily to School Council the training contents.

For Modern Information Engineering Enterprise Practice I at semester 6, Modern Information Engineering Enterprise Practice II at semester 7 and Undergraduate Thesis at semester 8, every student will be paired with a SISE teacher. Students are required to report weekly to their teachers for their periodic achievements. In this way, those students who didn't perform well and those companies who didn't provide good training to students will be identifiable timely. Necessary measures such as warnings on the students or moving the students out of the program will be taken.

3.5   Internship Summary and Company Grading

When the internship is finished, every student and every company will be required to write a summary for the internship. Considering performance of the student's altitude, ability and achievements, companies will give every student a score. The students with a score below standard will not get their undergraduate degrees.

3.6   Internship Project Defense

SISE encourages students to go to companies which have signed agreements with SISE. However, SISE also allow students to contact companies by themselves. On one hand, because the education plan was made only 4 years ago and the student population for SISE has been increasing since then, it is not easy to find a company for every student although SISE has signed internship agreements with dozens of companies. On the other hand, allowing students to go to companies not in the SISE company list give students better chance to find a position at their hometown or in a better company. The question left is how to control training quality for those at self-contacted companies. In addition to mandatory weekly report to SISE teachers, SISE requires every student to present their project achievements and do a project defense after they are back to school. A Defense committee of 5 experts will question and evaluate the achievements of the student and finally score the student's performance in the project. In such a way, students are prevented from taking chances and wasting their time by doing nothing.

4 Problems and Countermeasures

The education plan has been practiced smoothly at SISE for 3 years. On the whole, it has been very successful. However, there are still some problems to be dealt with.

4.1 Quantity and Quality of Cooperative Companies

More than 30 companies have been approved by School Council for internships. However, only nine companies provide internship positions in 2014 for SISE students and have comparatively close cooperative relation with SISE. Table 2 shows the number of students those companies recruit for the year of 2014.

As can be seen from Table 2, while there are 444 students in total that need to be placed at companies, SISE can only offer students nine different options. In addition, only two cooperative companies are multinational companies, while most cooperative companies are local companies at Chengdu.

Table 2 Distribution of students at companies

Company name	Number of students
Chengdu Dongfangtong High-tech company, Ltd	23
Changhong Group	44
Chengdu Weina software company, Ltd	51
Qingniu (Beijing) High-tech company, Ltd	50
UESTC Keyuan company, Ltd	31
Wensi Haihui High-tech company, Ltd	117
Daqing Jinqiao	3
Beijing IBM company	9
SAP company, Germany	23
Other companies	93
Total number	444

To solve this problem, SISE joins various societies and organizations such as Software Industry Association, Electronics Industry Association and Industrialization and Informatization Alliance for the purpose of establishing better connection with the industries. On the other hand, the first batch of students is now looking for jobs. Some students took job offers from companies at which they did their internship. It is very encouraging for companies to be a partner with SISE. They thought recruiting students for internship is a good way for them to make a reserve for their future employees. In a word, more and more companies become interested to recruit students from SISE for internship. Till the end of 2014, more than 30 companies have signed agreements with SISE for providing internship opportunities. It is foreseeable that SISE students will have more diversified and high-end choices for their internships in the near future.

4.2 The Unwillingness of Companies to Accept Students at the Undergraduate Thesis Stage

At the end of 2014, senior students at SISE started to contact companies for Undergraduate Thesis which is their final stage at school. However, although companies are very enthusiastic about recruiting students for Modern Information Engineering Enterprise Practice stage, they are very reluctant to recruit students for this last stage. Firstly, at this stage, most students pay more attention to finding a job than to participating in a project and they are quite uncontrollable at this stage. Secondly, companies think their engineers are not qualified to guide students to write a thesis. It is worth considering whether students should stay on campus and finish the graduate project and thesis under the guidance of teachers or they should finish Undergraduate Thesis at companies. To solve the problem, SISE now allows students to do Undergraduate Thesis on campus or off campus. If a student will do thesis at a company, a teacher will be assigned to guide him or her through this process to ensure the quality of Undergraduate Thesis.

4.3 Quality of Enterprise Cooperative Courses

Although SISE requires that the teachers for Enterprise Cooperative Courses to have practical skills and government granted title, it is not necessary that they could be good lecturers. From the feedback of students who took Enterprise Cooperative Courses, most course teachers are also good at teaching. Still some teachers are not serious or capable of being a course teacher. Next step, SISE will take several measures to ensure the quality of Enterprise Cooperative Courses. First, pre-post training will be initiated which requires every first time course teacher to go through a teaching skill training process. Secondly, their teaching materials including slides will be evaluated by School Council before the course starts. Thirdly, teaching evaluation system will take effect and those with bad evaluation will be forbidden to teach again at SISE. Even with these measures, it will take time for SISE to have a group of qualified enterprise course teachers to collaborate with.

4.4 Work Pressure on SISE Teachers

With a student population of more than 2000 and a teacher population of less than 100, the student teacher number ratio is more than 20, while the average student teacher number ratio of UESTC is about 9. The initial motivation of this setting for SISE is to hire more teachers from the industries or to hire more international teachers. If there are plenty of off-campus teachers, there is no need for having many on-campus teachers. The truth is that with limited budgets it is almost impossible to invite many off-campus teachers to teach at SISE. In addition, not like teachers at other schools of UESTC, in addition to teaching courses, SISE teachers have to take other tasks such as leading the summer holiday internship, guiding thesis writing and internship quality control. This situation cannot last for the long run. Luckily, the university realized these problems and made plans to allocate more resources for SISE. The university already offers more than ten million RMB for lab construction and extra subsidies to students for enterprise placements and overseas placements. Next step, the university plans to allocate more money and resources to SISE so that it is possible to hire more teachers from companies and overseas. Hopefully, the situation will get better in the near future.

5 Achievements

With the practice of the Outstanding Engineer Education Plan, SISE has witnessed fruitful results. Students have been very active in various competitions. Table 3 lists first prizes won by SISE students at national or international level competition.

SISE students are also very successful in job market. Until now, more than 95 % of those SISE grade 2011 students who decided to get a job immediately after graduation have signed 3 party agreement with SISE and companies which will hire them. Considering the percentage of those who will further their education, more than 98 % of SISE grade 2011 students know where they can go after graduation now. A group of four SISE grade 2011 undergraduate students acquired a five million RMB Venture Capital with their project named 'Location-based C2C Instant E-commerce' and they have already started a company in Beijing. They are the only undergraduate group at UESTC which manages to land Venture Capital while still at school.

Table 3 Prizes won by SISE students at competitions

Competition	Prize level and number
International Genetic Engineering Machine Competition held by MIT	Golden medal
ARM ST competition	One of the two first prizes
IBM mainframe Competition	Two of the five first prizes
Intelligent terminal design competition held by Baidu	The only first prize
SAP Lumira Competition	One of the two first prizes

6 Summary

The Outstanding Engineer Education Plan has been practiced at SISE of UESTC for more than 3 years. Generally speaking, it has been a very successful plan in respect of engineering education.

However, as the first batch of students in the plan is still on campus, there are quite a few problems to be dealt with for this new plan. With the support from the University, problems will be solved and Outstanding Engineer Education Plan will play its active role for cultivation of software talents.

The Construction for Quality Assurance System (QAS) of Training Professional Master of Engineering of University of Electronic Science and Technology of China

Xie Juan Wang Ye

As the scale of graduate students who pursuing the degree of professional master of engineering keeps increasing, the current crucial issue that training institutions need to consider carefully is how to deal with the relationship between the scale and the quality, and the very important work summarizes as follows: According to the objective and requirement of training, we are to improve the training system combining the characteristics of people who study for professional Master of Engineering so that we can build an effective QAS of training professional master of engineering. Quality of professional master degree student education is closely related with the scale of recruitment, the quality of student resources and the education model. Like many other Chinese universities, UESTC has recruited too many professional master degree students. For example, professional master degree student population exceeds 10,000 for school of information and software engineering at its peek. Most of the students study in the way of remote education. In addition, age and professional background of the students varies much. All these give much pressure to education process. So the quality Assurance measure are extremely important for professional master degree student education. These years, UESTC have made some beneficial exploration on the construction for QAS of training professional master of engineering, and formed the experience and practice such as follows: "around a core, the establishment of three mechanisms, making good use of the nine elements" (called the "139 way"). We will share it here.

X.J.W. Ye (✉)
University of Electronic Science and Technology of China, UESTC, Chengdu, China
e-mail: jxie@uestc.edu.cn; wangye@uestc.edu.cn

© Springer International Publishing Switzerland 2016
S. Kassel, B. Wu (eds.), *Software Engineering Education Going Agile*, Progress in IS, DOI 10.1007/978-3-319-29166-6_7

1 The Core We Around

We need focus on the objective of training professional master of engineering to change educational philosophy and plan educational work. The training of professional master of engineering focus on practice and application, and the goal is to train applications and complex high-level talents who can undertake independently an engineering technology or engineering management. As a professional for enterprise needs, the train of master of engineering requires students have both theoretical knowledge and practical ability, and can use the theoretical knowledge to solve practical problems. As the school side, it requires colleges and universities can apply the scientific research and the social demand together, and it is necessary to do a good job of teaching, improve scientific research, but also combined with social responsibility, focusing on market-oriented.

2 The Establishment of Three Mechanisms

2.1 The Assurance Mechanisms of Communication

One of the important influence factors of training quality for professional Master of engineering is the geographical characteristics. As a result of physical education, remote teaching and the students scattered in different places, How to realize the training points of school and out of school, effective communication among the student is particularly important. So we establish and improve the communication and coordination mechanism which the information platform, supervision of training and management of students in different places are included, through the integrated use of the advantages of the institution and technology. Based on the communication and coordination mechanism, we can guarantee interconnection and intercommunication of information, and all the main elements of the work are included into a closed-loop framework, which overcomes the natural deficiency caused by regional characteristics.

2.2 The Management Mechanism of Learning Cycle

We are guided by the education philosophy called "student-centered", focusing on the whole lifecycle management of the training, and conduct periodic planning based on the time scale. Ultimately, we establish a learning cycle management mechanism which includes customization of training program, teaching management, the proposal management and thesis management. And according to the characteristics of different teaching points and students' individual needs at each stage, this mechanism can set the key nodes, targeting to develop solutions that best meet students' needs, to achieve "suit one's measures to local conditions, and tailored". Through the flexible and lightweight roll management, we enhance the quality and efficiency of our training work.

2.3 Monitoring Mechanism of Quality

A necessary part about the contribution for QAS is to be fully effective implementation of supervision, and the purpose of supervision is to assess training quality scientifically, master the process dynamically and put forward reasonable suggestion. We formed a monitoring mechanism of quality which composed of the educational inspection system, the academic warning system and the feedback mechanism, and it can realize dynamic supervision for each training node, so that timely adjustment problems during training. Through this correction mechanism, not only can we ensure transparent and efficient learning cycle, also promote continuous self-improvement of our QAS.

3 The Good Use of the Nine Elements

3.1 Aspect of the Assurance Mechanisms of Communication

a. The construction of information platform.

We can establish information communication between school (college) and students through the information platform. Due to the particularity of the training professional master of engineering such as most teachers and students are not in the same place, so they can not communicate face in face, this produces a certain negative impact on the quality of training. And for changing this situation and ensure the quality of training, school and academies make full use of the Internet to contribute the information platform which organically combine of the teachers, students and administrators in different regions.

Academies establish the management platform of the dissertation stage training.

After finish the learning of course periodically, students can submit their dissertation proposals, interim reports and dissertations, they also can communicate with their teachers. Teachers can guide students' paper at any time in the information platform, such as propose amendments, so teachers, students and school administrators can grasp the progress and perform good interaction. After teacher audits the dissertations, administrator assignments teachers who responsible for reviewing the dissertations, and students can gain the results and amendments in the information platform. Because the use of the information platform, it sets up a bridge between teachers and students to produce closer ties between them.

School establishes the management information system of training stages.

The system can reflect the information of tutor assignment, course, the dissertation proposal, dissertation's situation in medium-term, the final defense of dissertation and final degree conferment. And training nodes out of school and administrators can query timely students' academic progress to facilitate the management of students and academic warning.

b. Monitoring mechanism of training nodes out of school.

Different from the traditional mode of education, the training of professional master of engineering requires school and local educational institutions work together, and the convey and execution of teaching management, student organizations and school-related Institution depend on the training nodes [1]. So, we gradually standardize the supervision of training nodes, defines the rights and obligations of both parties to strengthen the evaluation mechanism. And at the same time, we close the training nodes which can not reach the opening conditions, can not effectively organize students and mismanagement, so that ensure healthy and continual development of training nodes. In order to let the staffs of these training nodes achieve the requirements of our teaching management, we organize annual meeting to convey our policies in terms of training and training managers, also listen to the advice and demands of the training nodes to improve relevant regulations.

c. Remote students' daily management institution.

The administrators of training nodes make the institution of students' management, for example, regularly contact students by telephone, mail or another way to convey school-related policies, and institution of students and so on. Also, students can reflect their problems to school through the training nodes. In a word, training nodes is the bridge between school and students.

3.2 Aspect of the Management of Learning Cycle

a. Set up of training plan.

According to the characteristics of engineering and the requirements of enterprises, we set up the course related to Master of Engineering degree which Associated with the engineering field. For the project-oriented features, we optimized the course and the selection of textbook, and more focused on engineering applications [1]. Furthermore, we also strengthen the construction of teaching materials, and organize teacher to write a number of broad, comprehensive and high-level textbook related to the requirements of enterprises.

b. The management of teaching stage.

In order to ensure the quality of teaching that is the core of training, we strengthen our teaching staff to produce a number of great teachers with good virtue, a wealthy experience in teaching and development of engineering projects. In teaching, our teachers focus on interaction with students. And to fully mobilize the initiative of students and enhance students' ability to solve practical problems, they change in traditionally theoretical teaching mode and combine new field of knowledge engineering, new technology and engineering examples together.

We always put the quality of teaching in the first place, and require teachers must in strict accordance with curriculum schedule and can not reduced hours or change the teaching time by themselves, this put an end to the acts such as save teaching cost and compressed the time of class. Through evaluation of teaching and survey of training nodes, we master teachers' teaching and strengthen the management of teachers.

The way of the training stage of professional master of engineering always be remote teaching, due to the separation of space, the teaching always be centralized instruction form. And considering that the students are studying while working, it is difficult to guarantee the class time, so it must have some flexibility in teaching management. Before one semester, we would send the teaching plan and courseware to students so that they can arrange their time and learn in advance. For the students who can not finish their course in time because of their work, they can study with lower grades, other training nodes or the main campus. And only after getting the credits of training program requires, can students enter the stage of dissertation.

c. The management of opening and dissertation.

After getting the credits of training program requires, students can enter the stage of dissertation, and there always be experienced professional advice guide students about the precautions, which called opening guide. And after communicate with teachers, students can write their opening reports. It be double tutorial system, that is, a teacher of school side, a mentor of business side, and they guide title of dissertation jointly. There are strict regulations about the quality of the business side' mentor, which must be senior technical staff with relevant professional backgrounds who is in the first line of production and management and can guide students complete applied project. And the teacher of school side is familiar with the specification of dissertation, focusing on writing and horizontal of dissertation. The cooperation of the both teachers plays an important safeguard for the guidance of students' dissertation [2]. During the opening, professional review the students' opening based on the principle of responsibility for students. According to our experience, a successful opening can make a smooth road of graduation.

For ensure the quality of dissertation, we make a series of related rules and regulations to regulate strictly the work of opening, review and defense [3]. During the work of review and defense, it use "double-blind" rule which require the dissertation accepted by all teachers must remove the information of teacher and student to review by professional only based on the quality of dissertation, and both of the teachers who responsible for reviewing must propose a detail amendment for student to modify. Also, the dissertation that gain the two teachers' approve participate in the spot checks organized by the Graduate

School, which a experienced professional review the dissertation again, and only the dissertation that past the spot checks can enter final defense of dissertation.

3.3   The Monitoring System of Quality

a. Inspection mechanism

In order to improve the education quality of professional master of engineering, strengthen management of training process, promote the quality of education developing sustainably and healthy, we appointed a group of experts with rich culture, practical experience, and strong sense of responsibility, which composed the inspection team. Their mission is to assist the Graduate School supervising the education quality, and provide constructive comments and suggestions for the school on Graduate Education.

Firstly, the experts in inspection team will attend lectures of stage school in order to check the organization and implementation of the teaching plan, assess the content and quality of courses, supervise teachers' rules-broken activities and teaching accidents, inspect students' discipline and attendance, at the same time experts collect feedbacks which reflect teaching effectiveness from student.

Secondly, we check the opening report of graduation paper and supervising the dissertation defense are indispensable, inspect the organization and implementation for opening report and thesis defense will, in accordance with professional standards of master's degree about topic, content, innovation, workload, writing form and other aspects of dissertation norms ensure the thesis quality.

Thirdly, we supervise the tutors' dissertation guidance, check if tutors conscientiously perform their duties, inspect the implementation and practical guidance of experts offered by enterprise.

b. Academic warning system

According to state regulations, the enrollment status of professional master of engineering are 5 years, if someone don't finish his/her studies within 5 years, his/her enrollment status will be canceled. It is different from full-time master, the professional master of engineering master may delay their studies because of work, family or other reasons, resulting in can't graduate on time and enrollment status be canceled.

In order to improve the graduation rates, school established a academic warning system to make each college to master information of students about credit situation and graduation paper, thus warning defects. students whose study more than 3 and a half years will be reminded and warned, someone whose study more than 4-year will be urged by his/her tutor on thesis work, so that can graduate on time.

c. Feedback mechanism

School uses the telephone, email to get feedbacks from students, thus providing the basis for improving the quality of education and further rules and regulations. According student's feedbacks mainly relate to the teaching and

Table 1 The comparison of 2011–2014 year dissertation ratio

Year	Total	Pass	Degree granted	Rate (%)
2011	1700	1465	1432	84.2
2012	1768	1586	1531	86.6
2013	1793	1613	1593	88.8
2014	1874	1705	1676	89.4

learning progress, contact with mentor, training management, fees and so on, so as to know whether the students comprehend the training process, suggestions to mentors and school, students' feedbacks will be processed in time.

The above is the measures of professional engineering master's education quality guarantee system (called the "139 way") of University of Electronic Science and Technology of China (UESTC), with the development of the system, the quality of professional engineering master's education will be effective guarantee. Students are satisfied with courses setting, teaching management, defense specifications and school staff, fully affirmed the principle and effect of school.

The Table 1 below is the relevant data of UESTC, demonstration software college oral defense for graduation in recent 4 years:

From the above statistical data, although the number of students who apply for graduation reply increasing year by year, the degree granted rate increase steadily, in the past 4 years. To believe that with the development and execution of education quality assurance system of professional engineering master of UESTC, the training quality of professional engineering master of UESTC must be further improved.

References

1. JIN Xiao-hong. The Reflection on Issues of Cultivating On-Job Postgraduates in Different Places [J]. JOURNAL OF ZHEJIANG INDUSTRY&TRADE VOCATIONAL COLLEGE, 2010, Vol.10. No3:93-96
2. ZHOU Yue-jin. Quality management and control for Degree Theses by Part-times Master-of-engineering Students[J]. Journal of Graduate Education, 2014, No.4:75-80
3. Professional master degree management brochure of UESTC [Z]. CHENGDU:UESTC, 2014, 119-123

Exploration and Achievements of Students' Vocational Education of Software Engineering Major

Yan Zhao Zhang and Lei Hong

In 2001, in order to adapt to the social development of the information society era, meet the needs of information society for the majority of software professionals, and coordinated with the new industrialization road of "stimulating industrialization with Information technology" [1], the Ministry of Education established national demonstrative software colleges, aiming to cultivate internationally competitive multi-level practical talents with market demand as orientation. Therefore, the significance of cultivating students of software engineering major is evident. And the cultivation focus lies in the engineering education training. During the years of practice, the university and the college have also conducted continuous in-depth explorations, and achieved certain results.

1 Position of Student Cultivation Objectives of Software Engineering Major

Evidently, the core of software engineering major is the "engineering". The cultivation of students of software engineering major will also focus on the development of their engineering capabilities. But with the rapid development of information industry, and the ever-changing information technology, the cultivation of students' engineering capabilities has already not limited to the programming capabilities. It requires students having the abilities of advancing with the times, understanding the needs of the times, the community, and the enterprises, and creatively exploring more applied achievement. To say it informally, the cultivation of students of

Y.Z. Zhang (✉) • L. Hong
School of Information and Software Engineering, University of Electronic Science and Technology of China, Chengdu, Sichuan 610054, China
e-mail: zhangyanzhao@uestc.edu.cn

© Springer International Publishing Switzerland 2016
S. Kassel, B. Wu (eds.), *Software Engineering Education Going Agile*, Progress in IS, DOI 10.1007/978-3-319-29166-6_8

software engineering major is to cultivate more industry leading talents, rather than more programmers. However, the abilities needed by industry leading talents are more than technical abilities, but certain business acumen, management skills, communication and interpersonal skills. Therefore, the cultivation of industry leading talents is essentially to foster compound-type creative talents with certain humanistic quality, cross-disciplinary knowledge, and outstanding integrated ability.

At the same time, information industry is not a closed industry. Information technology is an important tool in promoting globalization. The Popularization and promotion of information technology is the foundation of promoting the internationalization process. Therefore, information technology has actually crossed the national boundaries, and become a worldwide universal "language". The cultivation of software engineering talent should also need to break the boundaries of the closed areas and step on the international road [2]. So integration, internationality, and applicability are the inevitable targets of software engineering student cultivation, which requires students able to work in software systems analysis design and development, project management, and maintenance and operation of software systems, and obtaining the continuous innovative motivations and quality in promote the software industry.

2 Exploration of Students' Vocational Education of Software Engineering Major

2.1 Cultivate Students' Practical Engineering Ability Based on Practical Training

Traditionally speaking, university is a kind of "research" unit, which talent cultivation should serve to the purpose of its "scientific research" to a large extent. Therefore, the emphasis on the student's academic ability, research capacity and theoretical level has long been the objective of various universities' talent cultivation. Admittedly, this traditional model has a positive meaning in promoting the national progress of science and technology, and the development of national defense. But with the deepening of China's reform and opening up, the continuous development of the socialist market economy and the constant progress of economic globalization, the social demand of shifting technology into productivity has been more prominent. In fact, only a small part of university students are engaged in scientific work. The vast majority of university students directly begin to work in society. Therefore, it is of vital importance to foster students' engineering practical abilities during the university. Especially in today's rapid development of information industry, the large gap of software talents and high demand are the basic feature in recent years. Thus, the cultivation of students' engineering practical abilities and enabling software engineering students to work after graduation has significant meanings.

The most important way of cultivating students' engineering practical abilities lies in the practical training. According to the cultivation requirements of "excellent software engineers", software engineering students should complete at least 1 year of internship within the 4 years of university. The purpose of the internship is not only to enable students to understand what companies are doing, more importantly to learn how to do in enterprises, and enable students to join in the enterprise projects, making the students have certain engineering ability. Therefore, students' practical training must be implemented: first of all, based on positions, it should strictly require students to engage in software development, software testing and other technical positions in the software industry, thus achieving the goal of improving students' engineering ability. Secondly, it should strengthen the practical assessment, actively communicate with the enterprise, understand the situations of students' internships and project participation in time and supervise strict attendance. Finally, it should assess the effect of student internships in internship defense, and requires students completing at least 1 year of internship with quality and quantity guaranteed.

2.2 Establish College-Enterprise "Business Class" Cooperative Model and Broaden Students' Knowledge Breadth

In the traditional university classroom teaching, although the teachers have certain research abilities and theoretical knowledge, most of them come from "old-type schools". They have long been engaged in theoretical research, and lack of program development and management experience. What they teach is mainly knowledge theory and latest academic studies, which put much more emphasis on academic hot point and technological problem, and fail to transfer the requirement of the enterprise and the market, resulting to the detachment of the knowledge from the market. This also leads to the difficulties of applying the knowledge by the students, and makes the enterprises to spend more costs in training new graduate employees. For example, the programming languages that are taught in universities are mostly C language and C ++. In fact, the programming language that enterprises really need is JAVA. Such knowledge dissymmetry is also the factor that causes the employment dilemma to a certain extent [3].

The form of enterprise cooperative class is to invite high-level personnel with rich program experience or engineering managers in the enterprises as "enterprise tutors" to go deep in the classes in order to discuss market leading edge with software engineering students, transfer the requirements of enterprises and society, teach related knowledge of enterprise program R & D and management, and provide enterprises' entrepreneurial work and management experience. The enterprise cooperative class is the important supplement of traditional theory teaching. What the enterprise tutors bring is not only the professional knowledge in enterprise program development, and more importantly, it is to transfer the thinking model of enterprise, which can enable students to make corresponding improvement on their technical capacities and other abilities specifically from the perspectives of enterprise and market, thus strengthening their competitive consciousness, stimulating their entrepreneurial passion, and promoting the improvement on their innovative capability [4].

2.3   Build a Platform for Innovation and Competition, and Encourage Students to Accumulate Project Experience

Program experience is of great importance for software engineering students. It will be a great help for students' internship and employment if there is certain program experience during universities. The purpose of the establishment of software engineering major is to cultivate students' with strong manipulative ability, practical experience and market orientation. Comparing to the traditional computer technology and science, theoretical learning in the classroom is not all the content. It can be seen that many students with excellent employment have such a path: the competition and program experiences accumulated during universities can enable students to go good enterprises for internship, which can help them to find good jobs. Therefore, it has significant meaning to encourage students to participate in competitions and programs.

The college holds various types of software design competitions, which are naming by enterprises, through directly providing projects and enterprise cooperation forms, encourages students to participate, and provides funds, places and teachers' support for students who participate in the projects, in order to create good innovative and entrepreneurial environment for students, and enable students to accumulate project experience in competitions and build up their manipulative ability.

2.4   Strengthen International Exchanges, and Expand Students' International Perspective

Software industry is not a closed industry. The globalization and internationalization processes mean that the breakthroughs of any software technologies are global technological breakthroughs, and the competitions in software industries are the competitions that are made in international platform. Therefore, the cultivation of students' engineering abilities must place them in the international platform. Only by enough international exchange and cooperation can expand students' international vision, make them understand the latest global market edge, and learn and grasp the most advanced technology and concepts, thus realizing the cultivation objective of internationalization.

The promotion of international exchange requires strengthening students' language ability, paying attention on the improvements of students' English abilities, and enabling them to have the basic English material searching ability, English material reading ability, and English system and software utilization ability, etc. in addition, it should constantly push the process of studying abroad, develop various forms of cooperation with universities in other countries, and carry out various foreign study exchange and cooperation programs as many as possible. Also, it should encourage students to exchange and study further in developed European and American countries, and expand the exchanges and cooperation with Asian software powers, like India, so as to enable students to make self-improvement in international view.

2.5   Carry Out General Education Courses, and Cultivate Students' Comprehensive Quality

As students of engineering, software engineering students have introversive characters. They have the ability of immersing themselves in work, and lack the communicative competence and humanistic quality, which have been the bottleneck that restrict them developing from "excellent" to "outstanding" level. What outstanding software engineers do is more than writing programs and solving technical problems. More importantly, they can lead and manage the whole enterprise teams and jointly promote and complete various projects. Also, they can thoroughly understand the market requirement through acute market sense, explore and develop more new projects which can satisfy social requirements. This must require them obtaining certain enterprise management knowledge and ability, organizing and coordinative abilities, and strong communication ability. Also, they should be equipped with economic mind and market awareness, and strong comprehensive quality.

Therefore, the cultivation of excellent software engineers must strengthen the cultivation of comprehensive quality of software engineering students. It should develop more general courses in class setting. In the required courses, besides the courses related to software, it should strictly examine the basic scientific courses, such as calculus, linear algebra, probability theory, and college physics; in the setting of elective courses, it requires students learning multiple courses on history and philosophy and other social sciences and art, music and other art appreciation courses [5]. Finally, it enables students to grasp the required technical and theoretical knowledge of software engineering major, including programming technique, system platform technology and software engineering approach, and massive knowledge base in mathematics, science and engineering and humanities and social sciences.

3   Achievements of Students' Vocational Education of Software Engineering Major

3.1   Student Employment Is Oriented with Market Demand. Signing Contract with Enterprise Has Been the Mainstream

The software engineering students also cater to the market demand in their employment process. Most graduates go to enterprises to engage in software research and development and other technical positions. Just few of them leave the software industry. Although the employment does not have a characteristic of diversification, such employment pattern is the inexorable outcome of engineering education. Students can apply their knowledge to the maximum extent, and bring their knowledge learned during university into working positions and play certain role. This conforms to the original intention of establishing the demonstrative software college, meet market demand with market orientation, and promote the development of national information industry.

3.2   Good Student Employment Quality and High Employment Platform

The software engineering students not only have good employment situation with high contact signing rate, also have higher initial salaries after graduation. Compared with students of other major, they have high average salary. The large number of high salaries is the basic feature of software engineering graduates. In one aspect, this can be attributed to the whole industry environment with urgent market demand of software talents. Also, it is contributed to the cultivation pattern of engineering education of software engineering. In the long period of practice and training, and with the possible international exchange, graduates have strong engineering abilities, and are equipped with certain market sense and international view. Once they are admitted in the enterprise, they can directly participate in projects, which save enterprises' training costs and improve corporate benefits to an extent.

Beside employment salary, the students have high employment platform, which earn better opportunities for future development. Quite a number of students work in China Telecom, China Mobile and other world's top five hundred companies, and Huawei and other hundred enterprises of china electronic information. Also, a part of students join in Alibaba, Baidu, Tencent and other tycoons in the industry.

3.3 Upsurge Entrepreneurial Passion and Striking Entrepreneurial Achievements

The introduction of entrepreneurial thought and the cultivation of comprehensive abilities improve students' engineering abilities and comprehensive quality, and also stimulate their entrepreneurial passion. Therefore, quite a number of students join in the entrepreneurial team, and entrepreneurial teams spring up constantly. The most prominent team has earned millions of venture investment during universities. And the majority of teams have been persisting in the entrepreneurial path.

Meanwhile, numbers of graduates open the special "entrepreneurial" path. They join in the small size entrepreneurial companies, which are just established, become the backbone of the company business, and follow the companies' entrepreneurial teams to start business.

After the continuous exploration, the college has found a characteristic path which is suitable for the talent cultivation of software engineering, which can improve students' engineering ability and comprehensive quality, and cultivate a batch of software engineering talents which meet the requirement of "outstanding plan". However, the path of exploration is just initiated. The college still has a long way to go in the talent cultivation of software engineering.

References

1. Guan Zhonghe. Thoughts on Applicable Talent Cultivation Pattern [J]. China University Teaching, 2010, (6):7-11
2. Zhou Yuanqing. Improving Quality is The Key Factor in Educational Reform and Development [J]. China University Teaching, 2011, (11):5-7.
3. Wang Xinhai, Li Jiandong, Li Jiena. Study on Software Engineering Course System [J]. Computer Education, 2011, (4):70-73
4. Xu Hongzhi. Reform and Practice of Software Engineering Talent Cultivation Pattern [J]. Computer Education, 2014, (22), 119-120
5. Wang Lin, Cai Jingye, Guan Qing, Lei Hang, Wu Zufeng. Exploration of Software Engineering Talent Cultivation Pattern based on "Outstanding Engineer Education Plan" [J]. Experiment Science and Technology. 2012, (6), 324-326

Joint UB-HIT Master: A Survey of Graduate Students

Yan Wang and David Chen

1 Introduction

University of Bordeaux (UB) and Harbin Institute of Technology (HIT) have launched in 2006 a joint master program on enterprise engineering and software engineering [1]. The objective of this program is to provide for the students all over the world a high level education environment both in the domain of enterprise engineering and software engineering [2]. The duration of this joint master is 2 years. The first year's courses in HIT put the emphasis on programming language, science and methodology and IT technique related to information system design and implementation, and the second year's courses in UB focus on enterprise engineering, production management, enterprise modeling, project management and interoperability.

As the crisis of the US subprime mortgage spread widely, the enterprise all over the world faces many economic difficulties. The financial problems in enterprise lead to the pressure of employment. How to solve the problem of the graduate students' employment becomes more and more urgent and difficult. In general, the government and society need the continuous development and creative enhancement. Moreover, through the analysis of graduate students, students can establish an objective for future employment and this will help to improve the study efficiency and develop a better learning plan in the university.

In this survey, 102 graduate students in total including 71 Chinese students and 31 international students have been taken into account. The main objective is to collect professional information of those graduate students and draw some general conclusions as the reference for the future students. To collect the information of graduate students, several communication techniques such as QQ, e-mail, WeChat,

Y. Wang (✉) • D. Chen
IMS, University of Bordeaux, 33405 Talence Cedex, France
e-mail: yan.wang@etu.u-bordeaux.fr; david.chen@ims-bordeaux.fr

© Springer International Publishing Switzerland 2016
S. Kassel, B. Wu (eds.), *Software Engineering Education Going Agile*, Progress in IS, DOI 10.1007/978-3-319-29166-6_9

Facebook, LinkedIn and telephone call were used for contacting those students. The contact message sent to the students includes a proposed simple questionnaire.

After this brief introduction in Sect. 1, Sect. 2 will give the main results of this survey. Section 3 points out some limitation of this survey and analysis. Section 4 will discuss about the future trend and perspective of this joint master program. The final conclusion will be presented in Sect. 5.

2 Overview of the Results

Table 1 shows the distribution on the origin (Chinese, French and others) of the students. The responses of 100 students were obtained including 19 international students (others than China and France) including Eastern Europe, Turkish, India, and Southeast Asia. Figure 1 shows the distribution of various communication techniques used through the survey. It indicates that email providing the highest amount to the total (46 %, 46 data) is the main method to contact the students. QQ provides the second high amount to the total (27 %, 27 data) just because it is the most used messaging software in China. LinkedIn also provides the 18 % (18 data) as it is widely used professional network. The remaining data resources provide: 1 % (1 data, Facebook), 6 % (6 data, telephone call) and 2 % (2 data, WeChat). Part

Table 1 Data analysis sorted by nationality

	Received number	Total number	Percentage over total
Chinese students	71	71	100
French students	10	10	100
Other foreign students	19	21	90.5
Total students	100	102	98.0

Fig. 1 Information extracted by communication technique

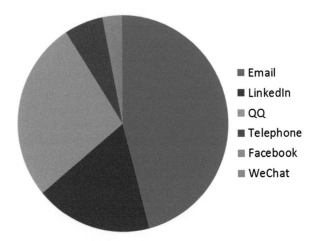

of the information on the employment and job position of some students were obtained indirectly (such as LinkedIn and Facebook). Also in some cases, one student can give information on several students he knows or in close contact with him.

Based on the analysis of the data of the graduate students, we have defined some criteria in eight different categories as below. These different categories cover all the data of the graduate students. The working places depend largely on the nationality of the students that are mainly sorted by Chinese, French and others.

- PhD study: This category includes the students who choose to study PhD or post Doctor in the colleges and universities.
- Colleges and university: This category covers the most of the students after the PhD study. It concerns teacher, manager and secretary working on the education services and academic research in the colleges and universities.
- Large companies: This category includes many kinds of the jobs but all focuses on the computer science and technology area. They are engineers, designers, managers and many different kinds of IT specialists in the international and big companies.
- SME companies: This category covers the students who join in the small and medium size enterprise and work in the computer science and technology area.
- Government employment: This category includes the workers who work for the civil service and it also includes the engineer and researchers who work in the government department.
- Entrepreneurship: This category includes the students who create/start a business or other organization under their own responsibilities.
- Non-IT companies: This category contains the students who choose a job which has no relationship with the computer science and technology.
- Unstable job: This category includes the internship student before becoming the formal employee in the companies and institutes. It also contains the unemployed and home-based students who are still searching for jobs.

Table 2 shows the job distribution of Chinese students. An important part of Chinese students continue their PhD study (16.9 %) after the joint master program

Table 2 Chinese students data analysis

	China		Other counties		Total in both places	
	Number	Percentage	Number	Percentage	Number	Percentage
PhD study	4	5.6	8	11.3	12	16.9
Colleges and university	6	9.9	5	7.0	11	15.5
Large companies	24	33.8	10	14.1	34	47.9
SME companies	1	1.4	0	0	1	1.4
Government employment	3	4.2	0	0	3	4.2
Entrepreneurship	1	1.4	1	1.4	2	2.8
Non-IT companies	2	2.8	1	1.4	3	4.2
Unstable job	5	7.0	0	0	5	7.0

study. Most of PhD studies are abroad (11.3 %) (France, Norway, Canada, Australia). We also found that 47.9 % of students after graduation work in large companies and an important part of them are in China (33.8 %), probably because a higher employment requirement is needed for students to work abroad. Language is also a main obstacle to find job in Europe (especially for non-English speaking countries like France, Spain, Italy, etc.). It is to note that the number of students who work in large company is much higher than those on PhD study. This is probably because that most of large companies are globalized worldwide and the good English speaking ability of the graduate students as well as their international study experiences are appreciated. It is also to note that a larger part of students work in industry is also in line with the objective of the master: to educate high level professional for international working place environment. It is interesting to remark that 15.5 % students continue to work as teacher and researcher at colleges and university after their PhD study. In the same way we also make an analysis for the French students and the other international students, it is obvious that most of French students prefer to stay in France than in other countries and other international students prefer to work in France than in their domestic countries. However due to the weak number of students investigated, this fact cannot be considered as a generalized conclusion.

Figure 2 makes a summary of the classification analysis for all the students. We can find that large company is still the most favorite choice and PhD study is the second. It can also be observed from Fig. 3 that PhD students decrease in the middle of the period but increase again in the recent years. This is because that University of Bordeaux has signed recently an agreement with CSC (Chinese Scholarship Council) to provide grants for the joint master students to continue a PhD study. The number of the students who take PhD study influences the number of students working in colleges and universities. Large companies are always in the first place of the choice except in 2008. Entrepreneurship is found in the beginning of the period but almost disappear in the recent years. Non-IT job position can only be seen in 2009 and 2011.

Fig. 2 Distribution of total students in eight categories

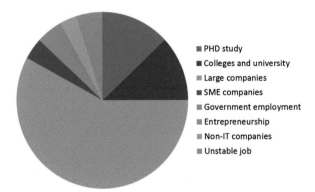

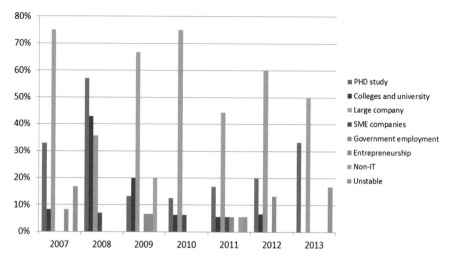

Fig. 3 Evolution of total students in eight categories

3 Limitations of the Survey

In this survey, the main problem is how to get precise and latest information from graduate students. The information from LinkedIn is not directly gained from face-to-face communication, the credibility and perceived correctness is sometimes not as high as expected. In order to get the real information we need to privilege direct contact techniques instead of LinkedIn, although this will cost more time to set up.

This survey is just an "instant photo" of the students in January 2015, changes will happen after this survey. A periodical update of the results is needed. As more and more students participate in this joint master program, this survey also needs to be updated regularly.

The survey presented is only a first preliminary investigation; it also needs to be refined. For example it is more interesting to know how many HIT students work at technical level and how many HIT students work at the administration level in the IT Company. The same refinement would be needed on the research area of PhD students (IT related subject or others).

Last but not least, it will be interesting and important to compare the results of the survey with the employment situations of HIT students graduated from HIT master program. The results of this comparison will allow better knowing the advantages or shortcomings of the joint UB-HIT master program, and providing recommendations to strengthen strong points and improve the weaknesses in the future.

4   Discussion

The joint master program provides a good opportunity for Chinese students to go abroad to study. The study is not only concerned with scientific and technique aspects, but also cultural and personal enhancement building. Indeed both Chinese and Europeans need to better know and understand each other in order to better develop their professional collaboration based on mutual trust and benefits.

The survey presented in this paper not only provides the places and return of experiences for collaboration education, but also more possibilities of finding international professional job positions. Relatively, this survey shows a big potential requirement for IT business market in China. We are sure that after reading this paper, more and more students will participate in this joint master program. And also the survey would help them to better establish their objective of study, either to continue a PhD study in foreign countries or work in large international companies in computer science area.

5   Conclusion

In this paper, a preliminary survey on the employment situation of the joint UB-HIT master graduates was presented. Information on 98 % of graduated students is covered by the survey. It has been shown that most of all students found a job after graduation. The survey concludes that continuing a PhD in Europe (and other parts of the world) and working in big companies in China are the two main trends. Although there were some difficulties in getting direct contact with some students, we believe that this limitation doesn't call in question the credibility of the results obtained.

References

1. Alix, T., Jia, Z. and Chen, D., Return on experience of a joint master programme on Enterprise Software and Production Systems, CEISIE'2009, Bordeaux, France, 25–26 May (2009)
2. Chen, D., Vallespir, B. and Bourrières, J.P., Research and education in Software Engineering and Production Systems: A double complementary perspectives, Third CEIS-SIOE, Dublin, Ireland, 6–7 February (2007)

Enhancing Computing Student Employability Skills Through Partnership Working in STEM Outreach

Scott Turner

This paper looks at an approach at the University of Northampton that involves:

- Linking but not combining a local STEM volunteering scheme to the National STEM Volunteers [1]
- Creation of a STEM Steering Group that has representation across all parts of the university.

Three brief case studies of computing student volunteers at different stages will be presented and culminate with a personal reflection based on observations over a 10 year period.

1 Introduction

Student volunteering is growing in the UK and elsewhere, in particular the UK government has been encouraging a wider uptake of volunteering and Universities have taken up the challenge (e.g. [2]). There is an ongoing debate about whether student volunteering is really "self-evidently a 'good thing'" and there is a need for reflection of whether this is true [3]. It is recognised that there is value to students volunteering, that includes, from an employability perspective, the student being able to try new things to clarify career options [4] and the idea of 'having something good to put on the CV'.

S. Turner (✉)
Department of Computing and Immersive Technologies, University of Northampton,
Northampton NN2 6JB, UK
e-mail: Scott.Turner@northampton.ac.uk

© Springer International Publishing Switzerland 2016
S. Kassel, B. Wu (eds.), *Software Engineering Education Going Agile*, Progress in
IS, DOI 10.1007/978-3-319-29166-6_10

2 Approach

Though volunteering within the University of Northampton has a relatively long history, this paper concentrates on the recent history (within the last 10 years) and the involvement of Computing staff and students.

2.1 Linked but not Combined

The University runs its own STEM Ambassador (recently changed to STEM Champion) scheme, which is separate to the National STEM Ambassador scheme [1] but with complementary goals. The separation allows the university scheme and its participants to have a little more flexibility and the University to have more evidence of where engagement has taken place. The programmes are very closely linked, with induction and training for the National scheme often carried out simultaneously at the University to local ambassadors. Based on the figures Sinclair et al. [2] of the 73 active STEM Champions, 42 are also active National STEM Ambassadors.

2.2 STEM Steering Group

Four years ago there was a recognition from within the University that there was STEM Outreach activity going on that was not being captured, lack of co-ordination of the activities and there was no formal mechanism to do this. A STEM Steering Group was set up, initially with three academics (from two schools in the university) and the person leading on Ambassador activities in the University, to organise and a few events organised. Since then the group has grown to over ten members from all over the University, with regular meetings, collaborative activities being carried out and training events organised. As well as members of staff there are also four other key members of the group—the local co-ordinator for the National STEM Ambassador, a member of the Student Union and two student STEM champions.

2.3 Computing's Part

The Computing staff team have been actively involved in STEM outreach activities from the beginning running and co-ordinating activities, such as robot programming (and robot building); Junkbots [5]; Women into Computing activities. Staff have supported students initially by students being involved in activities run by the staff; but for a small number of students by providing opportunities for them to run activities on their own. A few students even went on to create and run their own activities.

3   Case Study

Three brief case studies of example students are included below. They reflect the different levels of engagement (shown in Sect. 2.3) that students can undertake based on their confidence and interest. In the author's opinion it is important to work within what the students are comfortable with; for example Student A gradually became happier to create and lead her own events; whereas student B is enthusiastic and able but does not yet want to lead a whole activity on his own or create events. Both should be seen as acceptable and appropriate. As a point of clarity when a student in the case studies is described as being unsupervised what is meant is that they a leading the activity but there is always another responsible adult within the room to comply with the University guidelines on child safety.

3.1   Student A

This student graduated in 2011 from BSc Computing (Internet Technology and Security) course. During her time at University she ran and developed a workshop at a number of events to encourage women into computing. At one these events she went on to meet a member of the British Royal Family. Currently working as a software developer, she is also a part-time PhD student looking into the ways problem-solving is taught in secondary schools from the perspective of a computing professional.

3.2   Student B

A current third year student on the BSc Computing course. During his time as an ambassador, has worked with an experienced member of staff on delivering robot-based activities, in schools, with children ranging in age from 10 to 14 years old. Additionally, he has developed the confidence to run part of an activity on his own.

3.3 Student C

A second year BSc Computing (Software Engineering) student who has worked both supervised and unsupervised, delivering STEM activities. Alongside this he is an active member of the STEM Steering group, bringing a student perspective.

4 Results

Data suggest these activities may help students to progress. As an example the 73 registered University STEM ambassadors are 5.3 % [2] more likely to progress from 1 year to another compared to the university benchmark and very slight (not therefore statistically significant +0.2 %) more likely to graduate [2]. Comments from student STEM ambassadors include [2]:

> *"I now have a better understanding of employability and how it will help me"*
> *"It has helped me to be more confident"*

5 Personal Reflection

There is some value in computing students becoming involved in these forms of volunteering, especially from the perspective of increasing students employability. In two of the case studies A and B, it is felt, that the author has seen the students exhibit greater confidence levels after being involved in these forms of activities. It might be the way they are treated, as when they run the activities, the schools tend to treat them as the subject 'experts' providing skills the schools do not have in-house.

As has already been noted by some authors [3] more work is needed to establish the efficacy of student volunteering schemes. This applies to the champion or ambassador schemes and there effect on student success and employability. There are some questions that need to be answered:

> *How successful would these students have been without the STEM ambassador intervention?*

Anecdotally, based on student feedback and staff observation, participating as a STEM ambassador can help with students understanding of their own employability, and confidence. One area we have to be careful to consider in terms of employability is the idea that the students' only motivating factor is to enhance their CV. Though this will be a factor, and valid reason/benefit, in the decision to becoming involved in volunteering; this should not be seen as the only reason. Altruism and enjoyment, in the authors view, do play a part in why students participate and it should be remembered that the activities usually have a fun element to engage both the volunteers and the participants.

References

1. STEMNet (2015) Science, Technology, Engineering and Mathematics Network [online] Available at: http://www.stemnet.org.uk/ Accessed on: 24th January 2015
2. Sinclair J, Allen A, Davis L, Goodchild T, Messenger J, Turner S (2014) "Enhancing student employability skills through partnership working in STEM outreach; the University of Northampton approach " HEA STEM Annual Teaching and Learning Conference 2013: Enhancing the STEM Student Journey, University of Edinburgh, 30th April-1st May 2014
3. Holdsworth, C., & Quinn, J. (2010). Student volunteering in English higher education. *Studies in Higher Education*, *35*(1), 113–127.
4. Brewis, G., Russell, J., & Holdsworth, C. (2010). Bursting the bubble: Students, volunteering and the community. *Research Summary*.
5. Junkbots (2015) Junkbots [online] Available at: http://junkbots.blogspot.co.uk/ Accessed on: 24th January 2015.

Review of a Problems-First Approach to First Year Undergraduate Programming

Gary J. Hill

1 Introduction

Problem solving is not trivial [1] and is an important skill, central to computing and engineering. The paper aims to summarise the authors earlier research on a problems-first approach to programming (e.g. [2, 3]) to further emphasise the importance of problem solving, problem-based learning/project-based learning and the benefits of both physical and visual solutions.

The importance of linking the problem-solving robot activity and the programming assignment, whilst maintaining the visual nature of the problem, will be discussed, together with the comparison of this work with similar work reported by other authors relating to teaching programming using robots [4, 5].

The approaches discussed have been disseminated to colleagues, not only within the author's University, but also in Europe and internationally [2, 3, 6]. Development funding support has also been received [7, 8].

There are **four** core themes that can be drawn from this experience, considered to improve first year undergraduate programming:

- Problem solving
- Problem-solving-first/Problems-first
- Problem-Based Learning (PbBL)/ Project-Based Learning (PjBL)
- Physical to visual

What is evidenced in the research activities below, is how the teaching of problems-first has evolved through the design of a new module with assessments designed around a professional practice project/problem based approach with a pseudo client brief (with functionality and requirements) together with clear and

G.J. Hill (✉)
Computing and Immersive Technologies, University of Northampton, Northampton, UK
e-mail: gary.hill@northampton.ac.uk

© Springer International Publishing Switzerland 2016
S. Kassel, B. Wu (eds.), *Software Engineering Education Going Agile*, Progress in IS, DOI 10.1007/978-3-319-29166-6_11

explicit marking criteria. Explicit guidance was given to the students on examples of feedback from previous students on where their work could have been improved.

2   Background

The module discussed was designed, developed and introduced in 2001, and particularly the problems first and problem-based learning nature of the module has been adopted throughout the undergraduate and postgraduate curriculum, not only in Computing, but also within Engineering [9, 10]. The module is structured into two parts, 8 weeks (16 h) spent on problem-solving followed by 16 weeks (32 h) of visual programming in Java. The underlying approach is that as the module develops the focus evolves from general concepts of problem solving (e.g. brain-storming, functional decomposition) to solving problems based around robots, which increase in difficulty (but not necessarily in complexity). The module is first assessed by a robot-based project (50 %), which then leads into developing the same problem via a graphical user interface (GUI) in Java, which is finally assessed (remaining 50 % of module assessment). The visual nature of the subject being taught and the linkage of the assignments aid the development of the necessary skills.

3   Problem Solving

The author has suggested earlier [11] that, probably the most important skills a computer scientist or engineer must possess are those of problem solving, to the point where the role of computers as problem-solving tools is seen as increasingly useful [12]. These skills are highlighted in numerous benchmark and guideline statements for engineering and computing [9, 10, 13]. Problem solving is not trivial [1]. In fact, if one considers the cognitive domain within Bloom's Taxonomy [14] problem solving involves the high-level skills of synthesis, evaluation, analysis and applications and so it is, perhaps, not surprising that students often struggle in this area.

4   Problem-Solving-First

The approach discussed here focuses upon the development of problem-solving skills first and not on learning a new programming language from the outset. Therefore, initially, any programming is kept simple with the minimum of commands, with *objects* unknowingly used, as these are later introduced/learned during the programming stage of the computing module.

The author advocates the effectiveness/importance of introducing problem-solving concepts **before** programming concepts, therefore, the introduction of problem solving as a precursor to technical programming in Computer Science education.

The author has, since 2001, considered the 'evolution', 'realisation', 'optimisation' and ultimately the 'evaluation' that for undergraduate first year undergraduate Framework for Higher Education Qualifications (FHEQ) level 4 programming a problem-solving-first approach should be taken. Therefore, the hypothesis that, *'Problem solving should be taught first as a fundamental skill and then latterly the programming language can be used/taught as a tool for solving problems'*, originated during discussion at a Java and the Internet in the Computing Curriculum (JICC) Higher Education Academy (HEA) conference in 2001 [15].

The idea that problem solving was an important aspect of programming and should be taught within programming modules was only beginning to emerge through the JICC5 [15] discussions and through an IEEE Computer Society Association for Computing Machinery, Computing Curricula [16] report. Although the report:

"sought to identify curricular models that minimize the weaknesses of the programming-first approach by focusing on algorithmic and problem-solving concepts rather than the vagaries of language syntax" [16].

However, they suggested three alternative models:

breadth-first approach that begins with a general overview of the discipline, an algorithms-first strategy that focuses on algorithms over syntax, and a hardware-first model . . . [16].

Whereas the author proposed the problem-solving-first approach, as recognised in 2014 by Koulouri et al. [17] stating that:

evidence of the approach's value has been demonstrated by Turner and Hill [2007], who adopted it and reported positive student perceptions [17].

Most significantly Koulouri et al. [17] concluded, after a 4-year *"iterative methodological"* study that: *"teaching problem solving before programming yielded significant improvements in student performance"*.

5   Physical to Visual

5.1   Physical Robots

The author predominantly discussed [11, 18–21]) the teaching of programming and problem solving to undergraduate first year computing students, using robots and visual programming to emulate the robot tasks. In student interviews [6] two respondents reflected on their perceived benefits of using robots:

. . .it takes the concept of problem solving and places it into a physical and tangible domain. . . [6]

*It's easier to understand something if you can touch it and try it in real life, rather than
seeing it on a screen* [6].

The initial emphasis was on using physical robots and this work was recognised
[22] and been cited as an example of one of the two learning models (Problem-
Based Learning) in a suggested framework [5].

5.2   Visual Robots

Students had already commented [6] that:

*The visual nature helped to identify errors in the programming logic and made it easier to
rectify any errors made.*
It helps me think through a problem if I can visualise it [6].

Although, there had also been issues with limited access to physical robots,
therefore, alternative opportunities were introduced with the use of robot simulators
from 2012 using Greenfoot [23] although Microsoft's Robotics Studio [24] had
been investigated earlier [11]. The different experiences of a visual/virtual robot
against a physical robot have not been too noticeable, but the smooth transition
between the problem solving and the programming section of the module has
become improved due to the visual programming assignment partially emulating
the Greenfoot Graphical User Interface.

5.3   Visual Programming

Any discussion around the choice of appropriate programming-first language has
been avoided; as this has been discussed and debated extensively [17] within the
computing community with the debate reinvigorated each time a new language
appears. However, since 2001, with advances in visual programming the author has
consciously used Java to get the students producing graphical user interfaces
(GUIs) and visual programming at the earliest possible opportunity. The module
has been assessed by the production and documentation of a Java GUI/visual
application that emulated the robot problem introduced in the earlier problem-
solving sessions

6 Problem-Based Learning (PrBL)/Project-Based Learning (PjBL)

As in the problem-solving section the grades, feedback and engagement with the activity were consistently positive. The idea of linking the problem-solving and programming assignments, with the same task, was seen as a positive feature. One student made the explicit comment that they felt there was a good progression from problem-solving to programming. In addition, the students commented that they could take the ideas developed in one part of the module to the second part, thus evidencing clear transferability of skills.

The author considers a simple definition of Project-Based Learning is where a project/challenge is set from the outset, such that one Problem-Based Learning activity leads to another and the series of linked problems form the greater challenge or project.

Štuikys et al., [5] citied the authors work as supporting/demonstrating one of the two proposed learning models (Problem-Based Learning). However, it could be argued that the other model of Project-Based Learning should also be seen to be supported/demonstrated, but they recognise:

> there is a thin line among the models, nevertheless, we introduce them as slightly different teaching scenarios (in other words the models are integrated within the scenarios) [5].

Whether the module of Problem Solving and Programming is considered as either problem-based, project based or both, it is felt that active learning occurs, where active learning can be defined where students:

> must talk about what they are learning, write about it, relate it to past experiences, apply it to their daily lives. They must make what they learn part of themselves [25].

The author would consider their work [2, 3] so far to be Project and Problem-based Learning, to include active learning. The aspect of the Project-based module that is liked by the students is the incremental revealing/introduction of key programming concepts and skills alongside immediate reinforcement and application in the project-based visual/GUI assignment. Each topic delivered can be seen as a self-contained lesson (learning object) with the following attributes:

- Introduction, aim and objectives
- Concepts introduced demonstrated (with examples)
- Summary of the concepts (with additional formative exercises)
- Direct discussion, consideration, reinforcement and application to the project-based assignment. This not only reinforces the new concepts, but also illustrates the 'real-life' relevance to the problem. This aspect of the module can be seen as true project-based learning with "*integrated curriculum where one problem builds upon another...*" [26].

It is felt that this visual project-based learning approach (with the incremental reinforcement and application) to programming, adopted from the outset, and the transferability of the visual problem-solving to the visual programming task facilitates active learning. This should include student engagement, enjoyment, learning and, ultimately, the ability to see the relevance to software industry-oriented practices.

7 Conclusion

This short paper has attempted to review the approach adopted by the author since 2001 of problems-first and visual programming to first year undergraduates. The integrated approach can be subdivided into **four** core themes:

- Problem Solving
- Problem-Solving-First
- Problem-Based Learning (PbBL)/ Project-Based Learning (PjBL)
- Physical to Visual

The recognised importance of problem solving has been reiterated and the idea of problems first, supported by Koulouri et al., [17]. The experiences described here indicate that students liked the visual nature of the Problem Solving & Programming module and that this helped their skills, but also that the students appreciate the importance of these skills as they advance in academic level [6] with student satisfaction consistently over 90 %. Problem-Based Learning (PbBL)/ Project-Based Learning (PjBL) is further supported and advocated by Štuikys et al., [5] but the importance of active learning [25] should also be recognised. There has been an interesting shift from abstract to physical and finally the use of visual simulation of robots and visual programming.

The approaches discussed have been disseminated to colleagues, not only within the University of Northampton, but also in Europe and Internationally. It is difficult to measure the true impact of the approach of: problem solving; problems-first; visual robot simulation and programming, problem and project-based (active) learning, but these have all naturally become a key enhancement to Computing (and other) higher education disciplines.

References

1. Beaumont, C., & Fox, C.: Learning programming: Enhancing quality through problem-based learning. In: Proceeding of 4th Annual Conference of the subject centre for Information and Computer Sciences of the Higher Education Academy (pp. 90-95). Newtownabbey, Northern Ireland: Higher Education Academy (2003).
2. Hill G. J., Turner S.: Chapter 7: Problems First. In: Software Industry-Oriented Education Practices and Curriculum Development: Experiences and Lessons, M Hussey, X Xu & B Wu (Eds.), IGI Global, USA, pp 110-126, ISBN: 978-1-60960-797-5 (2011).

3. Hill, G., Turner, S. J.: Problems first, second and third. In: International Journal of Quality Assurance in Engineering and Technology Education (IJQAETE). 3(3), pp. 88-109. 2155-496X (2014).
4. Williams, A. B.: The qualitative impact of using Lego Mindstorms robot to teach computer engineering. In: Institute of Electrical and Electronic Engineering (IEEE) Transactions on Education, 46, 206 (2003).
5. Štuikys, V., Burbaitė, R., Damaševičius, R.: Teaching of Computer Science Topics Using Meta-Programming-Based GLOs and LEGO Robots. In: Informatics in Education - An International Journal (Vol12_1), pp125-142 (2013).
6. Kariyawasam, K., A., Turner, S., Hill, G.: Is it Visual? The importance of a Problem Solving Module within a Computing course. In: Computer Education, Volume 10, Issue 166, May 2012, pp. 5-7, ISSN: 1672-5913 (2012).
7. HEA-ICS Development Fund: HEA-ICS Development Fund [online] Available from: http://www.ics.heacademy.ac.uk/projects/development-fund/index.php [Accessed: February 2015] (2015).
8. HEA-ICS/Microsoft Innovative Teaching Fund: Developing problem-solving teaching materials based upon Microsoft Robotics Studio [online] Available from: http://www.ics.heacademy.ac.uk/projects/development-fund/fund_details.php?id = 88 [Accessed February 2015] (2015).
9. Adams, J. P., & Turner, S. J.: Problem Solving and Creativity for Undergraduate Engineers: process or product? In: International Conference on Innovation, Good Practice and Research in Engineering Education July 14-16, 2008, Loughborough, England, Higher Education Academy. 9781904804659 (2008).
10. Adams, J., Turner, S., Kaczmarczyk, S., Picton, P., & Demian, P.: Problem solving and creativity for undergraduate engineers: Findings of an action research project involving robots. In: International Conference on Engineering Education (ICEE 2008), Budapest, Hungary (2008).
11. Turner S., Hill G. J.: Robots in Problem-Solving and Programming. In: 8th Annual Conference of the Subject Centre for Information and Computer Sciences, University of Southampton, 28th - 30th August 2007, pp 82-85 ISBN 0-978-0-9552005-7-1 (2007).
12. Gallopoulos, E., Houstis, E., Rice, J. R.: Computer as Thinker/Doer. In: Problem-Solving Environments for Computational Science, IEEE Computational Science and Engineering pp 11-23 (1994).
13. Houghton, W.: How can Learning and Teaching Theory assist Engineering Academics? [online] School of Engineering - University of Exeter. Available from: https://www.heacademy.ac.uk/sites/default/files/learning-teaching-theory.pdf [Accessed: November 2015] (2004).
14. Bloom, B. S. (Ed.): Taxonomy of educational objectives. In: Handbook I: Cognitive domain. White Plains, NY: Longman (1956).
15. JICC5: Java & the Internet in the Computing Curriculum, Higher Education Academy (HEA) – Information and Computer Sciences (ICS) Conference, South Bank University, London, 22nd Jan, [online] Available from: http://www.ics.heacademy.ac.uk/events/displayevent.php?id = 127 [Accessed: February 2015] (2001).
16. Computing Curricula: IEEE CS, ACM Joint Task Force on Computing Curricula, IEEE Computer Society Press and ACM Press. [online] Available from http://www.acm.org/education/curricula.html [Accessed: February, 2015] (2001).
17. Koulouri, T., Lauria, S., Macredie, R., D.: Teaching introductory programming: A quantitative evaluation of different approaches. In: ACM Trans. Comput. Educ. 14, 4, Article 26 (December 2014), 28 pages, DOI: http://dx.doi.org/10.1145/2662412 (2014).
18. Turner S., Hill G. J.: The Inclusion of Robots Within The Teaching OF Problem Solving: Preliminary Results. In: 7th Annual Conference of the ICS HE Academy, Trinity College, Dublin, 29th - 31st August 2006, Proceedings pg 241-242 ISBN 0-9552005-3-9 (2006).

19. Turner S., Hill G. J.: Robots within the teaching of Problem-Solving. In: ITALICS, HEA-ICS, Volume 7 Issue 1, June 2008, pp. 108-119, ISSN: 1473-7507 (2008).
20. Turner S., Hill G. J.: Innovative Use of Robots and Graphical Programming in Software Education. In: Computer Education, Volume 9, May 2010, pp. 54-6, ISSN: 1672-5913 (2010).
21. Turner S, Hill G, Adams: Robots in problem solving in programming. In: 9th 1-day Teaching of Programming Workshop, University of Bath, 6th April 2009 (2009).
22. Gold. N.: Motivating Students in Software Engineering Group Projects: An Experience Report. In: Innovation in Teaching and Learning in Information and Computer Sciences 9 (1), 10-19. DOI: 10.11120/ital.2010.09010010 (2010).
23. Greenfoot: Teach and Learn Java Programming. [online] Available from http://www.greenfoot.org/ [Accessed: February 1, 2015] (2015).
24. Microsoft: Microsoft robotics studio [online] Available from: http://msdn2.microsoft.com/en-us/robotics/aa731520.aspx [Accessed: February 2015] (2006).
25. Chickering, A. W., Gamson. Z. F.: Seven Principles for Good Practice in Undergraduate Education. In: AAHE Bulletin 39:3-7. ED 282 491.6 pp. MF-01; PC-01 (1987).
26. Savin-Baden, M. & Wilkie, K.: (eds) Challenging Research in Problem-based Learning. Maidenhead: Open University Press/SRHE (2004).

The Lab Internship Alternative

Gianmario Motta, Kaixu Liu, Tainy Ma, and Linlin You

1 Introduction

As we noted in an earlier paper, top university should excel in Teaching, Research, Citations, Industry income, International outlook [1], in parameters as Employability, Facilities, Innovation, Access, Research, Teaching, Internationalization, or, finally, in ad hoc criteria concerning the subject [2]. However, for a graduate, employability is probably the critical factor. Employability implies not only quality teaching but also close relationships with enterprises. In short, a Software Engineering (SE) school should produce employable graduates for a variety of businesses, which range from systems integrators and large user enterprises to software houses, as we suggest in Fig. 1. Therefore, SE shall be viewed in a broader perspective of the software applications engineering, that encompasses Enterprise Architecture, Database, Service Engineering and alike subjects.

In SE master's degree, internship is a critical phase for employment. Under the Italian rule, the last 6 months of SE Master's Degree are devoted to the thesis. The thesis may reflect either a research project or an internship in an enterprise. Under Chinese rule, Master's degree requires at least one-year internship, with some variations among the universities.

Our paper compares enterprise internship versus lab internship and considers a specific aspect, i.e. the relation between development of knowledge and employability, i.e. their value for enterprises.

In this comparison, we assume the following tenets, respectively for enterprise and lab internship. Enterprise internships develop process knowledge, that refers on "how-to-do" a work, as it happens with training on the job. On the other side, lab

G. Motta (✉) • K. Liu • T. Ma • L. You
Department of Industrial and Information Engineering, University of Pavia, Pavia, Italy
e-mail: motta05@unipv.it; kaixu.liu01@ateneopv.it; tianyi.ma01@ateneopv.it; linlin.you01@ateneopv.it

© Springer International Publishing Switzerland 2016
S. Kassel, B. Wu (eds.), *Software Engineering Education Going Agile*, Progress in IS, DOI 10.1007/978-3-319-29166-6_12

81

Fig. 1 Employments areas
of software engineers
(qualitative)

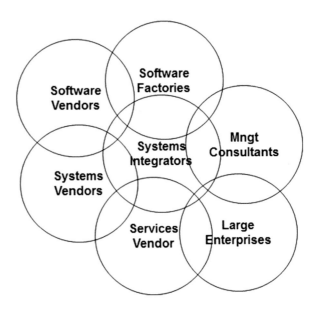

Fig. 2 Position of
enterprise internships
versus research theses

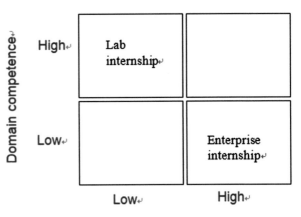

internships develop domain knowledge, which refers to the conceptual foundations
of a domain, e.g. system design or service design; domain knowledge is typically
acquired by participating to research projects. Domain knowledge results in high
value for the enterprises, who find not only labor ready but also state-of-art
knowledgeable candidates. Often a superior domain knowledge brings to higher
positions.

In Fig. 2 we represent these two axes of knowledge, and we have positioned
enterprise and lab internships. Enterprise internship has a higher value in process
knowledge and just a little one in domain knowledge, while lab internships have a
higher value in domain knowledge and a lower value in process knowledge. Indeed,
an enterprise internship hardly, if ever, can further enhance the conceptual abilities

of students. By contrast, lab internships can familiarize the student with advanced technologies and techniques. Enterprise internship is result-oriented, while lab internships provides more guidance and informal discussion among students in research theses, thus strengthening learning.

Our paper is structured as follows. In Sect. 2, we consider the issues of enterprise internship, based on analysis of the literature. In the Sect. 3, we discuss lab internship and we illustrate the case study of the IRMA lab project. Finally, we consider the outcome of the lab internship, and we conclude about the advantages, limits, and sustainability of the lab internship.

2   Critical Issues in Enterprise Internships

According to an opinion shared in both Europe and China, internships in enterprises are an optimal way to foster employment. Actually, these internships can develop a work experience. In most cases, they are seen by both universities and enterprises as a (almost) test period, i.e. a kind training on the job, where an enterprise can test the future employee. Last, not least, enterprise internships strengthen the links between universities and enterprises, a factor that is especially relevant for Software Engineering Schools in China, which aim at providing technicians, not researchers.

If we look at literature, internships play an increasingly important role in education with many advantages, ranging from applying theory, gaining experience and obtaining career-related direction [3]. However, considering that interns are temporary workers, fulltime employees may be reluctant to disclose important information to them [4]. In addition, many enterprise supervisors are too busy to provide effective supervision. Moreover, some employees regard interns as a threat to their position and, in some cases, supervisors possess lower qualifications than the students [5]. Interns look for inexpensive help and new ideas, while employees consider them only as a cheap labor force [6].

So what is the overall internship satisfaction level?

- "Most programs provide extensive field based experiences under the supervision of a practicing school counselor. These experiences are viewed very positively by counselor educators in terms of the practical preparation of students and in providing connections with counselors in the schools" [7].
- "There seems an emphasis on individual counseling with somewhat less attention devoted to group work and consultation, important components of developmental counseling programs"[8].

Internships enable students to accumulate real life experience, but they often lack a continuous tutorship. Moreover, effective internships require a careful selection of enterprises, assignments and students, and a concurrent quality control by university tutors. Projects in enterprise internships cannot thrive without a team spirit, and a substantial help from tutor.

3 Lab Internship in the Double Master Program

Lab internships has been and is extensively used in the Double Master's Degree (DMP) that the Computer Engineering School of University of Pavia is running together with Software Schools of Chinese universities, as HIT (Harbin), NEU (Shenyang), Tongji (Shanghai), UESTC (Chengdu). This experience is especially relevant, because it concerns both Chinese Software Engineering students and Italian Computer Engineering Students. Furthermore, it concerns an international class, taught in English. In order to better focus on the experience of Lab internship, we first illustrate the philosophy of DMP; subsequently we illustrate the profile of our lab internship.

3.1 Double Master Program Courses

DMP provides a double degree, i.e. Italian and Chinese. In DMP, Chinese students spend the first year in their home university and the second year in the University of Pavia. Conversely, Pavia's students spend one term of the first year in a Chinese partner university. Chinese students attend a class together with regular students who are enrolled in Pavia's Computer Engineering School. A typical class is about 15–20, and is really international: most students are not Italian, and teaching is totally in English.

DMP students attend a Service Engineering track, which follows a project-oriented approach. The four main courses of the track, which totals 24 European teaching credits, combine conceptual foundations and team project, as we illustrate here below, and address the main families of intranet and internet applications, that include, respectively, Enterprise Systems (ERP, BI, CRM) and Service Systems (Fig. 3). Most lectures are allocated to overview domain issues and illustrate design and modeling techniques. In order to reinforce these foundations, students are assigned a project in small teams. Exam marks typically reflect 1/3 the team's assignment, 1/3 its oral defense and 1/3 theory.

Such twofold foundations-project approach intends to nurture both the design ability (= capability of implementing what has been conceptually modelled) and teaming (= ability of work in a team). Both these skills are keys for lab internship, and, of course, for enterprise internship as well. Students begin internships in the second term of the second year. Someone choose enterprise and others lab internships. In Table 1, we describe the lab internship.

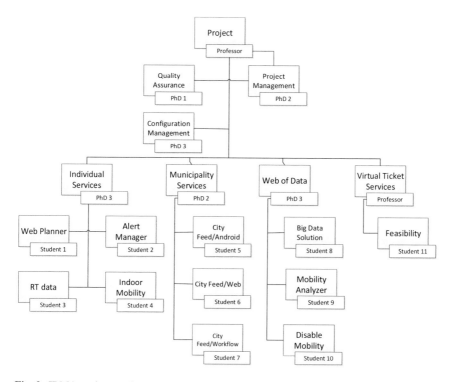

Fig. 3 IRMA project work team

Table 1 Profile of the main DMP courses taught in Pavia University

Course	Foundations	Team Project
Design of Enterprise Systems	• Architecture of Enterprise Systems: ERP, CRM, BI	• Design of the BI system of a service company
	• Techniques for conceptual modeling of BI systems: SIRE [9], DFM [10], GOA [11, 12]	• Design and demo of a dashboard on O/S software
Customer Relationship Management Systems	• Components of CRM Systems: Sales, Customer Service, Marketing, Analytical CRM	• Design and demo implementation of a Sales System
	• CRM platforms	
Business Analysis & Service Design/Module 1	• Business Process Modeling techniques and frameworks : BPMN [13], SCOR [14, 15], UML-EP [16]	• Modeling of a Business Processes (Industrial Enterprise)
	• Galbraith's Star Model on Organizational Design [17]	• Analysis and re-design of a Business Process (Service Enterprise)
Business Analysis & Service Design/Module 2	• Architecture and design of Service Systems	• Design and implementation of a value proposition (Smart City)
	• Implementation model and platforms for Service Systems	

4 Lab Internship

Lab internship is based on a student team that works on developing a demo within a research or business project. Projects in 2012–2014 included a Planning/Analysis system for Phonetica, a company running an elite call center [18, 19], Mobile Healthcare, Analysis of Psychiatric Patient Reports, and finally, IRMA [20], that we describe later. The student's internship lasts 6 months (sometimes longer for Italian students). In internship, students work in small teams, which are tutored by a PhD student. Teams report to the professor who supervises the overall project.

IRMA (Integrated Real-time Mobility Assistant) is a project for smart mobility, that includes a wide range of information services for citizens and municipalities. It was born as a thesis on a traveler's support system, and then was continued as a pilot for Pavia municipality. Two pilot releases, namely on Trip Planner and City Feed [21], a crowdsourcing system, proved its practical viability. These releases led to a contract with a Province of Pavia and the Smart City Lab of CINI (a consortium of Italian Universities), to a joint lab agreement with HIT and the School of Software of UESTC. Finally, a Chinese version of City Feed is to be deployed in Weihai municipality, by HIT. Of course, IRMA implies a quite large team, of up to 15 people.

In lab internships, the outcome is a demo. Sometimes the demo is robust enough to be released as a beta version. Actually, Phonetica is using the Planning/Analysis system. As noted earlier, some modules of IRMA are released on the websites of our Lab (http://camellia.unipv.it/servizi) and of Pavia Municipality. The City Feed module is daily run by Pavia Municipality. The contact with real customers—enterprises or public bodies—develops in students the experience of dealing with users' positions.

In lab internships, each team gives periodically progress presentations, which are discussed in project meetings. Of course, the lab internship requires a very intensive tutorship by the professors and PhD students, who spend 30 % of their time in discussing and supervising the teams.

4.1 DMP Thesis and Internships

As far as Pavia University is concerned, the thesis reflects a research project. Typical sections include:

1. Introduction, that illustrates context and objectives of the overall project and the goals of the module developed by the student;
2. State of Art, that includes a systematic literature review [22], that discusses the main researches on the topic, thus positioning the novelty of the thesis itself;
3. Analysis of Requirements, that models user needs, functional and non-functional requirements;
4. Design of the System, that describes both its overall architecture and modules;

Table 2 Profile of some lab internship theses

Student	Thesis title	DMP	Employer	Sector	Remarks
1.	Mobility support systems for people with physical impairment	NO	Atos, Milano	IT/Systems Integration	Employee
2.	Design & implementation of a web system to support indoor map conversion and refinement	Tongji	Atos, Milano	IT/Systems Integration	Employee
3.	Design and implementation of event awareness trip plan platform	NO	Alibaba, China	IT/Software Engineering	Employee
4.	Design & implementation of a workflow management system for City Feed	NO	BIP, Milano	Consulting	Employee
5.	Design & implementation of a crowdsourced business intelligence system for city management (Web module)	UESTC	Qunar	Product Manager	Employee
6.	Design & implementation of a crowdsourcing system for municipal administration (Android module)	HIT	University of Pavia	Academy	PhD student
7.	Design & implementation of a local event detection system using geo-tagged Twitter data	HIT	SOHU, Beijing	IT/Software Engineering	Employee
8.	Design & implementation of an urban public transportation simulation and analysis system	HIT	No	No	No
9.	A Platform for City Data Integration and Alert Manager with Social Media Data (Point of Interest)	NO	Politecnico Torino	Academy	PhD student
10.	Design and implementation of public transit open data service platform	UESTC	SAP, Shanghai	IT/Systems Integration	Employee
11.	Design & implementation of a mobile BI system for a call center	HIT	University of Pavia	Academy	PhD student
12.	Mobility Analysis for Smart Cities: Territorial Intelligence and Big Data	HIT	IBM Italy	IT/Systems Integration	Employee
13.	A platform for cognitive psychotherapy analysis	HIT	BIP	Consulting	Employee
14.	Design & implementation of a municipal crowdsourcing system (Web)	Tongji	Tongji/Pavia	Academy	Master student
15.	Design, Development & Prototyping of an APP for Patient Health Record	PV	IBM Ireland	IT/Systems Design	Employee

5. Deployment and Implementation, that illustrates how the design is implemented;
6. Test, that illustrates experimental results and discusses the validity of the design and implementation;
7. Conclusions, that illustrate the results achieved and related limits, and it outlines future work on the same subject;
8. Demo, which is also the base of the defense.

From the above description, you can easily understand that, in Pavia's Computer Engineering School, the thesis is assessed on its novelty and results. This approach, that reflects the research orientation of Computer Engineering, may conflict against the punctual protocol of Software Engineering Schools. In addition, Italy legally requires at least 6 months of internships (of course the internship may last longer), while China requires 1 year. To deal with these differences, thesis are separated, even if 50–70 % of the material is common.

The Pavia's orientation to research issues and design of systems is evident in Table 2, which lists the subject of lab internships, in 2012–13 and 2013–14 academic years. Several key words of these theses, as "Mobility", "Crowd-sourced", "Big Data", "Indoor Mobility", closely reflect current IT challenges, and give students competences that are very attractive for future employers.

The jobs of graduated students relate to their thesis. Among 15 graduates, ten work in multi-national companies, as Alibaba, IBM, and Atos, while four graduates work in academy, including three PhD students and one Master student. Only one graduate is still seeking a fulltime job. Admittedly, lab-internships result helpful for students. In addition, they enhance the ability of University to perform projects for corporations and public funding, while still keeping the control of the knowledge.

5 Conclusion

We have discussed a case study of lab internship and shown that it can be effective not only for the university, that uses research results of the students' work, but also for the enterprises, who receive a superior product. In short, lets us recap some positive points:

- Lab-internships provide a close guidance to students. 'Team spirit and involvement', and 'autonomy and help from superior' were influential factors in predicting students' satisfaction in internship [6];
- Lab internships enable the university to test ideas, while keeping the control of knowledge;
- In our case, lab internships enabled to shape a design capacity that goes from user needs all the way down to the implementation and test;
- Students learn how to work in teams, where each member performs a work package, that should match with other work packages;
- Students are encouraged to search solutions and literature on Internet, acquiring an autonomy that is really a key for higher level works

- Frequent visits, exchange of techniques and project experience with partner enterprises and partner universities help development of talent.

However, lab-internships are not a universal solution, because:

- Supervision costs are high–in our experience, over 20 % of PhD students and 10 % of professor time;
- A project-like organization is needed, and should run regularly, with plans, progress review and walkthroughs;
- Effectiveness and efficiency are high with high performing students, while low performers produce poor outputs and impact on supervision costs;
- PhD students may be not adequate mind to guide a team and should be supported.

So, as a last conclusion, the lab-internship complements enterprise internships, and fits schools and labs who participate in advanced research projects, and fits best students.

References

1. http://www.timeshighereducation.co.uk/
2. http://www.topuniversities.com/qs-stars/rating-universities-specialist-subjects-qs-stars
3. Muhamad R, Yahya Y, Shahimi S, et al.: Undergraduate internship attachment in accounting: the interns perspective. International Education Studies, vol. 2(4): pp. 49 (2009)
4. BUKALIYA, R., Region, M. E., & Marondera, Z. I. M. B. A. B. W. E.: The potential benefits and challenges of internship programmes in an ODL institution: a case for the Zimbabwe Open University. International Journal on New Trends in Education and Their Implications/www.ijonte.org. (2012).
5. Rothman, M.: Lessons learned: Advice to employers from interns. Journal of Education for Business, vol. 82(3), pp. 140–144. (2007)
6. Lam, T., & Ching, L.: An exploratory study of an internship program: The case of Hong Kong students. International Journal of Hospitality Management, vol. 26(2), pp. 336–351. (2007).
7. Gatling A P. Investigating the Impact of Field Verses University-based Science Methods on Preservice Teachers' Belief and Abilities to Design Inquiry-based Science Instruction for Diverse Learners. Boston College, (2010).
8. Corey G. Theory and practice of group counseling. Cengage Learning, (2011).
9. Motta, G., & Pignatelli, G. From strategic to conceptual information modelling: a method and a case study. In Information Technology and Innovation Trends in Organizations (pp. 179–186). Physica-Verlag HD. (2011).
10. Golfarelli, M., Maio, D., & Rizzi, S.: The dimensional fact model: a conceptual model for data warehouses. International Journal of Cooperative Information Systems, vol. 7(02n03), pp. 215–247. (1998).
11. Motta, G., Pignatelli, G., & Roveri, P.: Stakeholder oriented analysis for information intensive applications: a case study. ICIS 2009 Proceedings, 113. (2009)
12. Van Lamsweerde, A. Requirements engineering: from system goals to UML models to software specifications. (2009).
13. http://www.bpmn.org/

14. Huan, S. H., Sheoran, S. K., & Wang, G.: A review and analysis of supply chain operations reference (SCOR) model. Supply Chain Management: An International Journal, vol. 9(1), pp. 23–29. (2004).
15. http://www.apics.org/
16. Eriksson, H. E., & Penker, M.: Business modeling with UML. Business Patterns at Work, John Wiley & Sons, New York, USA. (2000).
17. Kates, A., & Galbraith, J. R.: Designing your organization: Using the STAR model to solve 5 critical design challenges. John Wiley & Sons. (2010).
18. Motta, G., Barroero, T., Sacco, D., & You, L.: Forecasting in multi-skill call centers: a multi-agent multi-service (MAMS) approach: research in progress. In Service Science and Innovation (ICSSI), 2013 Fifth International Conference on pp. 223–229. IEEE. (2013, May)
19. Barroero, T., Motta, G., & Della Vedova, M.: Right Sizing Customer Care: An Approach for Sustainable Service Level Agreements. In 2011 International Joint Conference on Service Sciences. pp. 40–43. IEEE. (2011, May).
20. Motta, G., Sacco, D., Belloni, A., & You, L.: A system for green personal integrated mobility: A research in progress. In Service Operations and Logistics, and Informatics (SOLI), 2013 I.E. International Conference on pp. 1–6. IEEE. (2013, July)
21. Motta, G., You, L., Sacco, D., & Ma, T.: City feed: A crowdsourcing system for city governance. In Service Oriented System Engineering (SOSE), 2014 I.E. 8th International Symposium on pp. 439–445. IEEE. (2014, April).
22. Biolchini, J., Mian, P. G., Natali, A. C. C., & Travassos, G. H.: Systematic review in software engineering. System Engineering and Computer Science Department COPPE/UFRJ, Technical Report ES, vol. 679(05), pp. 45. (2005)

An Exploration of MOOC + SPOCs Teaching Mode

Dechen Zhan, Chengjie Sun, and Xiaofei Xu

1 Introduction

Massive Open Online Courses (MOOC) is a kind of distance education which was first introduced in 2008 and emerged as a popular mode of learning from 2012 [1]. The emergence of MOOC is due to the development and popularization of network technology and computer technology. With MOOC, learners can easily access the best higher education resources in the world through network according to their own foundation, needs and time. Thus MOOC is helpful to eliminate the education imbalance. Currently, the most influential MOOC websites in the world arc Coursera, edX and Udacity. In China, there are two important MOOC website: one is "xuetangX",[1] which was launched by Tsinghua University; the other is "Chinese University MOOC (CUMOOC)"[2] which was built by Chinese Ministry of Education and Netease Company.

By using MOOC, ordinary people can easily gain access to higher education resources and college students can have opportunities to enjoy high quality courses from the most famous universities in the world. So MOOC can prompt the higher education reform. However, MOOCs can't meet the requirements of classroom teaching in higher education in its current form. The reasons include: (1) MOOCs are open to the society, so the content of MOOCs need adjust to attract the learners. But there is a contradiction between the learners' attention and the difficulty degree of the content. More difficulty usually leads to less attention. Reducing the difficulty of a course content to draw more attention can't achieve the goal of classroom teaching in higher education. (2) The huge number of audience, the various

---

[1] http://www.xuetangx.com/

[2] http://www.icourse163.org

D. Zhan • C. Sun (✉) • X. Xu
School of Computer Science and Technology, Harbin Institute of Technology, Harbin, China
e-mail: dechen@hit.edu.cn; sunchengjie@hit.edu.cn; xiaofei@hit.edu.cn

© Springer International Publishing Switzerland 2016
S. Kassel, B. Wu (eds.), *Software Engineering Education Going Agile*, Progress in IS, DOI 10.1007/978-3-319-29166-6_13

backgrounds of the audience and the different needs of the audience make targeted teaching impossible in one MOOC course. (3) The drop-out rate is very high in MOOCs because most learners are self-motivated in a loose learn manner [2]. It's hard to carry out effective teaching management in a MOOC course as in classroom teaching.

In order to let MOOC play an important role in the practical teaching of colleges and universities, we have to find ways to overcome the above problems. SPOC (Small Private Online Course) is a new way to use MOOC in classroom teaching. It builds a network classroom for a corresponding college class. This network classroom can share all the resources of assigned MOOCs and add specific teaching resources for the college class. Thus it can adjust the teaching content according to the needs of students in actual college class. It's also convenient to carry out teaching managements in SPOCs because their audiences are same as students in college classes. In this paper, we (Harbin Institute of Technology, HIT) explored how to use MOOC + SPOCs in practice. "College Computer" course was chosen as our carrier. HIT collaborating with other 11 universities in China practiced MOOC + SPOCs teaching mode for more than 16,000 students in 2014 fall semester. Our practice indicated that "MOOC + SPOCs" teaching mode can combine MOOC and actual classroom teaching in higher education. This mode can take full advantage of high quality MOOC resources, easily supply specific teaching content and carry out teaching management. So "MOOC + SPOCs" has potential to be a new teaching mode in higher education.

2   Why MOOC + SPOCs

2.1   Relations Between MOOC and SPOCs

SPOCs need to be built on the basis of high quality MOOCs. The content of the chosen MOOC course should be benchmark, which means the all the teaching contents have been included with necessary depth and breadth requirements. Thus the MOOC audiences who are willing to learn can learn more and the MOOC audiences whose learning foundations are not good can learn solidly by watching the content repeatedly.

In classroom teaching, teaching methods and requirements should be different for students with different foundations. For example, more contents may be taught for student with good foundations than for students with poor foundations within the same time span. So teachers for SPOCs need to choose MOOC contents according to the foundation of the students in the classrooms. Compared to MOOCs, SPOCs are more specific in teaching content, teaching methods and teaching management.

One MOOC can support many SPOCs and the teaching contents of SPOCs must be based on the contents of the assigned MOOC in order to keep the quality of the courses. This also indicated the benchmark function of MOOC in "MOOC + SPOCs" mode. The content of MOOC can guarantee the teaching quality in the situation where the teaching level are different in different universities and prompt the realization of education balance. The specific settings in SPOCs can realize differentiating teaching and characteristic teaching, which will fully mobilize the enthusiasm and initiative of teachers and students.

2.2 Teaching Difference for Different Types of Learners

As shown in Table 1, the teaching activities are different for learners from society and learners from colleges. MOOCs are suitable for learns for society, but can't meet the teaching requirements for college students. With SPOCs, the teachers can know the students better and afford better teaching services. In practice, students in each SPOC usually correspond to actual classes in colleges in order to provide targeted teaching content and carry out detailed teaching managements such as homework management and attendance management.

2.3 MOOC + SPOCs Improve the Teaching Effect

"MOOC + SPOCs" is a kind of teaching means to promote the teaching effect of higher education. It takes advantage of the MOOC platform to support the university teachers' teaching work and teaching administrators' work.

1. MOOC + SPOCs is a platform for teaching resources aggregation and utilization
   MOOC + SPOCs can aggregate all kinds of teaching resources and teaching achievements, including: (a) short teaching videos; (b) course learning guidance documents; (c) slides or PPTs; (d) exercises and answers; (e) discussion topics; (f) problem sets and tests; (g) text books et al. With MOOC + SPOCs, these aggregated resources could be utilized efficiently.
2. MOOC + SPOCs is a platform to support teaching works

Table 1 Teaching activities difference for different types of learners

Aspects of teaching activities	Society learners	College learners
Openness	Public and open	Private, only for students in the classroom
Requirements	Self-control	Mandatory
Supervision	Indirectly supervised	Directly supervised
Students Background	Various	Simple and similar
Teacher Responsibility	Teachers are free from responsibility	Teachers has responsibility for each student

Teaching works involve many aspects, including: the students' learning progress understanding, personalized teaching, diversification of assessment and individual assessment. These aspects are also import parts in teaching reform. Finishing these works need heavy workloads. MOOC + SPOCs mode can automatically collect and process and calculate the necessary data by platform, which can reduce routine workloads of teachers and support their teaching works.

3. MOOC + SPOCs is a platform to support works of teach administrators

Teaching process management is emphasized in higher education. Teaching evaluation and improvement are based on the data generated by lots of teaching activities. Currently, many data collection and statistics are completed manually. With MOOC + SPOCs, data can be aggregated automatically. Faculty and staff are disentangled from manually data collection and processing. Besides, these data are recorded and saved in a more detailed and completely manner than previous. For example, the learn activities of every student in every minute are saved in MOOC + SPOCs platform. The big data of high education is generated in this way. The usages of these data are important not only for teaching administrators to make correct decisions but also for teachers to improve the teaching process.

3 "MOOC + SPOCS" Practice in Cumooc Platform

We have known MOOC + SPOCs can be useful in higher education so for. The next question is how to do? In the following, this paper will introduce a MOOC + SPOCs practice on "College Computer" course in CUMOOC platform.

3.1 Challenges in Teaching Reform of "College Computer" Course

"College Computer" course, previously called "Computer Culture Foundation" and "Computer Application Foundation", has many arguments about its course contents. Currently it is agreed that its content should be dominated by computational thinking. More and more teachers and students realized that it is computational thinking playing an important role for students' innovative thinking in the future [3], not the usages of typical software or basic understanding of program languages. The contents of "College Computer" course should include: the relations between manually computing and automatic computing; how to implement automatic computing, computing system and program; how to write and compile and run programs; how to solve problems by computer algorithms, the fusion of computing, society and nature; network and data-driven thinking etc [4–6].

Although the contents of "College Computer" course have been clearly defined, there exist contradictions among "foundation, course contents and class hours". "Foundation" refers to that the audiences of "College Computer" course are freshmen and their computer foundations are different. "Course contents" refers to that it's difficult to choose teaching contents from so many contents related to computational thinking. "Class hours" refers to that there are limited hours given to "College Computer" course in the curriculum setting of non-computer majors.

The contradictions result in many problems, such as teaching goal is not clear, teaching materials are more about facts and less about thinking, teaching contents are shallow and excessive popularization, using terms to explain terms and concepts to explain concepts etc. These problems lead to people have wrong understandings like the level of "College Computer" course is low and "College Computer" course does little to students.

The contradictions also results in teaching administrators and teachers concern about the risks of teaching reform. The concerns of teaching administrators include: whether the students expect the new contents; whether the teachers have the abilities to teach new contents; whether the student can accept the new teaching mode. The concerns of teachers include: whether they have the abilities to teach new contents; what the risk of teaching evaluation is; whether the added workload is worthwhile; etc.

From the perspective of the teaching modes and teaching methods, this work used MOOC + SPOCs to resolve the contradictions: building high quality MOOC course and specific SPOCs based on the MOOC course. By this way, teaching contents can be reformed and improved; the overall level of teaching can be upgraded; and the thoughts of teachers and teaching administrators can be changed; the concerns of teachers and teaching administrators can be eased. The practice of MOOC + SPOCs carried out by HIT and other 12 universities in 2014 fall semester shown that the MOOC + SPOCs solution is effective.

3.2 MOOC + SPOCs Practice for College Students

The authors and their teaching team firstly opened a MOOC course "College Computer—an introduction to computational thinking" on CUMOOC platform from 2014-05-20 to 2014-07-15. In the course, the contents were elaborately divided into 15 lessons. Each lesson is about 120 min and was separated into several sections. Every section corresponds to a short video with 10–15 min. The content of a section is self-contained. There are connections among sections and all the lessons form a system. The course also provided enough test sets (about 50 questions per lesson) and discussion topics (four topics per lesson) for online test and discussion.

More than 9000 learners joined the course. Most of them are from society. Their occupations cover science and technology, medicine and agriculture, social sciences, the humanities and so on. The academic degrees of the learners include high school students, college students, post-graduate students etc. Some college teachers also chose the course to improve their teaching abilities. At the end of the course, about 1500 people participated in the final examination and 300 of them obtained the course completion certificates.

Based on previous MOOC course, the authors and their teaching team opened MOOC course "College Computer—an introduction to computational thinking" on CUMOOC platform for the second time from 2014-09-10 to 2015-01-15. At the same time, the teaching team collaborating with 12 universities firstly opened their own SPOCs on CUMOOC based on the MOOC course and started the MOOC + SPOCs teaching practice. Teaching resources, assignment/test and discussion area were divided into two parts in each SPOC: MOOC content area and SPOC specific content area. The two parts were integrated into one interface, so it's very convenient for learners to use. The SPOC specific content area was created and maintained by teachers of the SPOC, while the MOOC content area of all SPOCs shared the same MOOC course.

A typical SPOC content area included: a course announcement which explained the relations among MOOC, SPOC and classroom teaching, the learning content for the students belong to the SPOC and how to obtain the score of the SPOC; some specific discussion topics such as "what is your ideal teaching style in MOOC + SPOC mode" and "what is your feeling of your first MOOC + SPOC class". Some complex SPOCs reorganized the teaching plan based on the MOOC course according to the actual situation of students, designed specific requirements and created new courseware, problem set and homework.

The MOOC + SPOCs learners consisted of about 3500 students from HIT, about 3000 students from Nanjing University of Aeronautics and Astronautics, about 6000 students from Southwest University of Science and Technology, about 1700 from HIT Weihai, and students from other universities (including Hefei University of Technology, Harbin Engineering University, Northwestern Polytechnical University, Northeast Forestry University, Harbin University of Commerce, Qiqihar University, Hunan Normal University and Suzhou University of Science and Technology). Totally more than 21,000 students joined in our MOOC + SPOCs practice.

3.3 Evaluation for MOOC + SPOCs from Students

In order to assess the teaching effect of our MOOC + SPOCs practice, an online investigation was carried out. The respondents are MOOC + SPOCs learners from 2014 freshmen of HIT. The call for participation was published through MOOC + SPOCs online forum. The investigation contained 15 questions which was launched on 2014-12-16 and closed on 2014-12-20. The final collection included 348 results.

Following are some conclusions by analyzing the investigation results: (1) Most of students like MOOC + SPOCs teaching mode, only 16 % respondents chose "not like". (2) More than 65 % respondents think that MOOC + SPOCs teaching mode can improve their interests in learning. (3) More than 90 % respondents are willing to continue to accept MOOC + SPOCs teaching mode for the study of subsequent courses, and are willing to recommend this mode to other students. 4) Although most of teaching contents have been online, 56 % respondents think the classroom teaching is still very important when using MOOC + SPOCs teaching mode. Some respondents suggested the classroom teaching need adjustment like spending more classroom time to explain problem set. 5) Network speed, the layout of MOOC platform and the convenience to access the Internet have directly impact to the effect of MOOC + SPOCs teaching mode.

In order to fully evaluate the effect of MOOC + SPOCs teaching mode, more investigations need to be done, such as making comparisons on completion and attainment rates of face-to-face, MOOC + SPOC and MOOC only; analyzing differences between different participating colleges and checking correlations between SPOC access and student success. We will work on these issues in our further work.

4   Conclusion

This paper explored a new teaching mode called MOOC + SPOCs to bring MOOC into classroom teaching of higher education. To use the teaching mode in a course teaching, a high quality MOOC course needs to be built first. Then many SPOCs can be built based on the MOOC course.

In MOOC + SPOCs teaching mode, teachers' importance is not reduced, on the contrary the role of teachers may be more important. Many new works need to be done in classroom teaching, such as guiding the students to watch the course videos in SPOCs, inviting the students to attend the discussions in course forum and spending more time to explain problem sets.

With MOOC + SPOCs, many teachers can work together to build one course, which would enrich the course content, diverse the teaching methods, characterize course content interpretations. So MOOC + SPOCs can also promote course quality and benefit students finally.

The authors and their teaching team collaborating with 12 universities put MOOC + SPOCs teaching mode into practice on "College Computer" course. CUMOOC platform supported the practice. We can draw following conclusions from our practice: (1) MOOC + SPOCs can effectively connect the MOOC and classroom teaching and show its advantage on scale and platform. (2) MOOC + SPOCs can aggregate all kinds of good teaching resources easily and avoid repeatedly works. (3) MOOC + SPOCs can keep the characteristic of each SPOC on the basis of expanding consensus by sharing MOOC course content. (4) MOOC + SPOCs can realize the interactions between online and offline and interactions among universities. (5) MOOC + SPOCs can automatically accumulate and analyze teaching data. These data are valuable for teachers to improve teaching level and for teaching administrators to make correct policies.

Acknowledgment We would like to thank all the teachers and students attending our MOOC + SPOCs practice and the software engineers of CUMOOC platform who strongly supported our practice. This research was supported by Harbin Institute of Technology under Grant No. HIT20140134.

References

1. Pappano L. The year of the MOOC. The New York Times, Nov 2, 2012: ED26.
2. Lori, B. et al. 2013. Studying learning in the worldwide classroom: Research into edx's first mooc. Research & Practice in Assessment. 8, 2013, pp. 13–25.
3. Jeannette M. Wing. Computational Thinking. Communications of ACM, 2006, 49(3): 33–35.
4. Dechen Zhan, Lanshun Nie, Xiaofei Xu. "College Computer"—a computational thinking general education course need to be learnt by all college students. China University Teaching. 2011, (4): 15-20. (In Chinese) 战德臣, 聂兰顺, 徐晓飞.《大学计算机》–所有大学生都应学习的一门计算思维通识教育课程, 中国大学教学, 2011, (4): 15–20.
5. Dechen Zhan, Lanshun Nie. The basic idea for reform of computational thinking and college computer course. China University Teaching. 2013, (2): 56–60. (In Chinese) 战德臣, 聂兰顺. 计算思维与大学计算机课程改革的基本思路, 中国大学教学, 2013, (2): 56–60.
6. Guoliang Chen, Rongsheng Dong. Computational thinking and college computer foundation education. China University Teaching. 2011, (1): 7–11. (In Chinese) 陈国良, 董荣胜. 计算思维与大学计算机基础教育, 中国大学教学, 2011, (1): 7–11.

Documentation During System Development: Maturity Levels for Decision-Making

Alexander Rauh, Wolfgang Golubski, André Pflüger, and Chris Rupp

1 Introduction

There are various reasons for documenting knowledge in a development project e.g. to transfer this knowledge between different members or to keep it over a longer time. Nowadays, especially in the context of agile projects, the decision which information need to be documented is difficult. The following statement of the manifesto for agile Software Development might support the opinion that documentation isn't necessary and that the members of a project should spend their resources in run able and working software only:

Working software over comprehensive documentation [1]

However, in practice there is more than one reason for documenting knowledge in a project. For example, every person forgets information over time, which may be relevant in the future [2]. Documentation helps to keep knowledge over a longer period. Furthermore, while documenting knowledge the human brain can understand difficult dependencies between the single parts of a system and can work more efficient as described in [3]. Due to the limited capacity of the human brain [4], project members can use documents as an additional buffer of information to see the system as a whole.

The goal of this approach is to satisfy the people who are involved in the system development and not to be conform to the restrictions of a process model e.g. the V-Modell XT [5]. With such restrictions on the documentation the members don't

A. Rauh (✉) • W. Golubski
Westsächsische Hochschule Zwickau – University of Applied Sciences, PSF 201037, 08058 Zwickau, Germany
e-mail: alexander.rauh@fh-zwickau.de; wolfgang.golubski@fh-zwickau.de

A. Pflüger • C. Rupp
SOPHIST GmbH, Vordere Cramergasse 13, 90478 Nürnberg, Germany
e-mail: andre.pflueger@sophist.de; chris.rupp@sophist.de

© Springer International Publishing Switzerland 2016
S. Kassel, B. Wu (eds.), *Software Engineering Education Going Agile*, Progress in IS, DOI 10.1007/978-3-319-29166-6_14

have a choice to decide against documenting knowledge and have no variation points. The approach presented in this paper aims at process models with fewer restrictions and many points for variation e.g. in Scrum [6].

To decide which information should be documented in a development project, the following questions are relevant: Who needs which information when in which quality?

2   Making Decisions for Documentation

The first step to answer the questions above is to define who needs the knowledge in a development project. The focus of the documentation is the members who cover a role during the development of a system. The problem is that these roles differ from project to project and from company to company. The solution for this problem is to address the disciplines within a development project, which define these roles to avoid misunderstandings e.g. in the definition of a role. The five disciplines System Requirements, System Design, System Construction, System Testing and System Maintenance of the Software Engineering Body of Knowledge (SWEBOK) [7] and the people who fulfill these disciplines are used as recipients of the information in a project. The tasks of each of these disciplines are described in detail in [7].

The second part of this approach is to elicit which information are required while developing a system. The focus of this paper is on requirements engineering and lists especially clusters of information which are essential for the work of a requirements engineer. Important information for requirements engineering are extracted from [8]. Table 1 shows the relevant information and their content.

To answer the question aimed at the quality of knowledge, this approach defines maturity levels to rate which discipline requires which information for solving the discipline related tasks during system development. These maturity levels include attributes of knowledge and the states of these attributes.

The first of these attributes is the solidity of an information, which derives from the aggregate states of requirements. *Solidity* explains how precisely an information can be described for the transfer between people. In the *gaseous* state an information cannot be explained for knowledge transfer and must be extracted using techniques for elicitation from requirements engineering [8]. The *liquid* state describes that knowledge flows easily from person to person but is not documented yet. Information in the *solid* state can be accessed easily.

The second attribute is completeness. *Completeness* describes how much information on data are available within a defined context. The states for this attribute are *small parts* e.g. a vision about one functionality of the system. The state *essential parts* of the attribute completeness describes that the scope of one fact for a defined context is available, but there are some details missing. If the scope of certain data is clear and all details are available to the project members, an information is considered *complete*.

The degree of consolidation explains, if the knowledge is the result of a joint development of all relevant people in the project's context. *Consolidated* information are the result of a joint development with a potential higher quality than *not consolidated* knowledge.

Table 1 Types of information focused on requirements engineering

Information	Short description and content
Goals of the system	Describe the intention of the system
Context of the system	For the system development relevant environment of the system e.g. neighbor systems
List of stakeholders	Information to the stakeholders, which are the source of requirements to the system
Assumptions	General establishments, which are relevant for the people involved in the project
Definitions of terms	Describe the meaning of terms, which are used when talking or writing about the system
Business processes and rules	Describe activities of the companies, which are necessary for the integration of the system in these companies
Information model	Conclusion about important terms and relations between these terms including the structure of data
Functionality	The functional requirements to the system
Non-functional requirements	Requirements, which describe the quality of functionalities and the system as a whole
Acceptance criteria	Expectations of the customers to the systems or parts of it
Interfaces	Information about interfaces to neighbor systems in the context
Human machine interface	Describes the design of the human machine interface e.g. style guides for the layout of the graphical user interface
Handling of errors	Facts and context about errors and solutions for these errors

The attribute *validity* describes in which context of the project an information is obligatory. An information is *individual valid*, if the context of validity is only a part of the whole project e.g. a single person or a small group within the project. An *obligatory* information is valid for all people within the projects context.

The former described attributes are summarized in three maturity levels to rate which discipline needs which information in which quality. The *first maturity level* means that an information includes only gaseous and small parts, that are not consolidated and individual valid. Knowledge in this maturity level is only exemplary available and underlies a high rate of changes. The transfer of knowledge in this maturity level between people involved in the project is difficult.

Information at the *second maturity level* are liquid and include essential parts of this fact. These information are constant over a longer term and underlie less changes. The transfer of information in the second maturity level between members of the project is more easily. Knowledge in the second maturity level is not consolidated and individual valid.

The *third maturity level* is the highest rating in this approach. Information at this maturity level are solid, constant and include the scope of a fact with all relevant details. Furthermore, this knowledge is consolidated and obligatory for all people within the project. To reach the third maturity level, the documentation of the information is required because the techniques of consolidation need documented knowledge to succeed.

Table 2 Disciplines and the required maturity levels for the information

Discipline needs information in the maturity:	SWEBOK Knowledge Area's				
1: Exemplary, not consolidated to					
3: Complete, consolidated	System Requirements	System Design	System Construction	System Testing	System Maintenance
General					
Goals of the system	3	3	–	3	3
Context of the system	1	3	–	3	3
List of stakeholders	1	–	–	–	3
Assumptions	1	2	–	–	–
Definitions of terms	1	1	1	1	1
Business processes and rules	3	–	–	–	–
System					
Information model	–	3	3	3	3
Functionality	–	2	3	3	3
Non-functional Requirements	1	2	3	3	3
Acceptance criteria	–	–	–	3	–
Interfaces	2	2	3	3	3
Human machine interface	–	2	3	3	3
Handling of errors	–	–	–	–	3

Table 2 shows all parts mentioned in this paper. The table illustrates which discipline needs which information in which maturity level. The presented rating is the consolidated result of the experience of the consultants of the SOPHIST GmbH from many projects. The rating in the table is a reference and may differ from your own experience.

How to read this table?—For example, the discipline System Requirements needs the "Goals of the system" in the maturity level 3. The goals have to be consolidated and obligatory before starting with the project because these data define the direction of the whole development. To start with the elicitation of requirements before reaching the third maturity level is risky because the goals may change.

3 Conclusion

This approach shows how members of projects could be supported in making decisions which knowledge needs to be documented and in which cases the documentation is useless. This solution is a generic template which must be adjusted to individual project conditions. The content of Table 2 can be adjusted to the individual requirements depending on the situation in the project. For example, the disciplines in the columns can be replaced by roles for a concrete project. The list of information in the first column gives an overview about the most relevant information and can be expanded. Also the maturity levels in the table can be adjusted to the individual situations in a project.

References

1. Cunningham, Ward (2001): Manifesto for Agile Software Development. Retrieved from http://agilemanifesto.org/, last visited on 2013-07-31.
2. Cherry, K. A. (2007). Forgetting. Retrieved from http://psychology.about.com/od/cognitivepsychology/p/forgetting.htm, last visited on 2015-02-19.
3. Baddeley, Alan (2012): Working Memory: Theories, Models, and Controversies. Department of Psychology, University of York. York. Retrieved from http://sunburst.usd.edu/~schieber/psyc792/workload/Baddeley2012.pdf, last visited on 2013-07-02.
4. Miller, George A. (1955): The Magical Number Seven, Plus or Minus Two Some Limits on Our Capacity for Processing Information. American Psychological Association. Retrieved from http://www.psych.utoronto.ca/users/peterson/psy430s2001/Miller%20GA%20Magical%20Seven%20Psych%20Review%201955.pdf, last visited on 2013-06-28.
5. Federal Republic of Germany (2004): Fundamentals of the V-Modell. Retrieved from http://v-modell.iabg.de/index.php?option=com_docman&task=doc_download&gid=47, last visited on 2015-02-19.
6. Schwaber, Ken; Sutherland, Jeff (2013): The Scrum Guide. The Definitive Guide to Scrum: The Rules of the Game. Retrieved from https://www.scrum.org/Scrum-Guide, last visited on 2014-02-24.
7. IEEE - Institute of Electrical and Electronics Engineers (2013): Software Engineering Body of Knowledge (SWEBOK). v3. Retrieved from http://www.computer.org/portal/web/swebok/home, last visited on 2013-05-25.
8. Pohl, Klaus; Rupp, Chris (2011): Requirements engineering fundamentals. A study guide for the Certified Professional for Requirements Engineering exam: foundation level, IREB compliant. 1st ed. Santa Barbara, CA: Rocky Nook (Rocky Nook computing).

A Study on the Education Quality Assurance System for Master of Software Engineering

Kaikun Dong and Dianhui Chu

1   Introduction

Since Harbin Institute of Technology (HIT) and other 34 universities had been granted to establish national pilot schools of software by the National Ministry of Education and State Development Planning Commission in 2000, the education of Master of software engineering in China has been through 15 years. Great progress has been made and a large number of high level personnel of software engineering have been trained to meet the extremely increasing requirement from software industry [1]. However, some quality problems have also arisen in the education of Master of software engineering.

- In some universities, the postgraduate course system of Master of software engineering has a much overlap with that of Master of computer science, technology or engineering. The course content, teaching methods and teachers are similar to each other. Their course system has no much characteristics of software engineering.
- The quality of industrial practice is not high. In some universities, steady-going practice bases have not been established and no strict regulations have been set up to check and evaluate the quality of student's industrial practice and the quality of bases' running. Some students just take the industrial practice as practical experience before employment and no high quality of software development tasks have been accomplished.
- In some universities, the quantity and quality of faculty and other supporting conditions cannot meet the rapid growth of the number of students.

K. Dong • D. Chu (✉)
School of Computer Science and Technology, Harbin Institute of Technology, Harbin, China
e-mail: chudianhui@vip.sina.com

© Springer International Publishing Switzerland 2016
S. Kassel, B. Wu (eds.), *Software Engineering Education Going Agile*, Progress in IS, DOI 10.1007/978-3-319-29166-6_15

- The dissertations of Master of software engineering in some universities lack of engineering characteristics. On the other end of the scale, some dissertations are more like an engineering document but an academic thesis for a master degree.
- The education of Master of software engineering in some universities lacks of international visions.
- Some training units take the education of Master of software engineering as a way of creating income. Therefore, the quality control is lax during the educational sections such as the admission of students, course teaching and test, industrial practice, dissertation and giving degrees.

Quality is the lifeline of the education of Master of software engineering. To solve the problems mentioned above and assure the educational quality, an education quality assurance system for Master of software engineering is studied.

The rest of the paper is organized as follows. Section 2 investigates and summarizes the competency of Master of software engineering required from software industry. In Sect. 3, the education quality assurance system for Master of software engineering is proposed and Sect. 4 draws conclusions.

2 Competency of Master of Software Engineering

The achievement of educational goals is the aim of setting up an education quality assurance system for Master of software engineering. The competency requirements of high level personnel of software engineering have been investigated [2]. The respondents include technical and human resource directors from software enterprises, Masters of software engineering who have graduated and been worked in software industry, graduate student, teachers, educational administrators and specialists.

The competency of Master of software engineering required from software industry can be summarized as knowledge, skill, ability and other characteristics four aspects, as shown in Table 1 [3–6].

The knowledge requirements are the very foundation of the competency of Master of software engineering, which include knowledge breadth and depth of software engineering, and the acquaintance of general process of software engineering.

The professional skill requirements are the professional technical assurance of the competency of Master of software engineering, which include advanced programming skill, logical thinking capability and engineering practice ability.

The abilities requirements include process capabilities and consciousness abilities. The former covers communication, collaboration, coordination, practical problems analysing and solving abilities, and leadership, professional ethics, business and management, market development and adaptability capacities. Consciousness abilities requirements assure good international and social consciousness, self-

Table 1 Competency indicators of Master of software engineering

Competency aspects		Indicators	Requirements
Knowledge		Breadth of software engineering knowledge	Over-all knowledge structure and the acquaintance of software engineering related professional knowledge.
		Depth of software engineering knowledge	Mastery of knowledge of specialized application technologies or fields
		General process of software engineering	Acquaintance of international and national norms and standards for software engineering
Professional skill		Advanced programming skill	Acquaintance of algorithm analysis, design and optimization, not only coding
		Logical thinking capability	Capacity of correct and reasonable observation, comparison, analysis, synthesis, abstract, summarization, deduction and judgement
		Engineering practice ability	Capacity for applying acquired knowledge, technologies, modern tools and equipments in software engineering practice
Abilities	Process capabilities	Communication and presentation skills	Oral and written communication and presentation skills for communication with other people
		Ability of analysing and solving practical problems	Ability of correct analysing problems and difficulties encountered in software engineering practice, solving the problems and overcoming the difficulties using multiple methods through different ways
		Team collaboration ability	Emphasis on teamwork, collaboration ability, playing his/her own part in team working, and improving the work efficiency of the whole team
		Abiding professional ethics	Abiding professional ethics of software industry, honest and credible
		Business and management ability	Abilities of engaging in external economic and business affairs and internally software project management
		Leadership	Abilities of thinking all-sidedly, systematically and prospectively from the angle

(continued)

Table 1 (continued)

Competency aspects	Indicators	Requirements
		of leader, concerning about industry trends, determining the direction of enterprise development, finding a variety of ways of encouraging and coordinating people to take more efforts in achieving the global goals
	Ability of Market development	Abilities of accurate judging of market trends, excavating the new demands of market, acquiring new customers and expand the product market
	Adaptability	Abilities of dealing with the rapidly changing of new technologies and competitive environment, basically correct judging and responding to the emergencies
The consciousness abilities	International and social consciousness	Realisation the impact of international and social environment on software engineering, thinking software engineering problem under international and social backgrounds
	Self-consciousness	Accurate understanding and evaluation of personal condition, behaviour and activities, Self-regulation of one's thinking, feeling and behaviour
	Consciousness and ability of lifelong learning	Having a strong thirst for new knowledge and technologies, ability of lifelong learning
	Innovation consciousness and ability	Having innovation consciousness, thinking and ability
	Service consciousness	Trying his/her best to meet the demand of customers
Other characteristics	Toughness	Being stoical under the pressure of work tasks and various difficulties
	Dedication and responsibility	Having lofty ideals, driving ambitions, strong working enthusiasms and sense of responsibility and competition, being brave in exploring and developing
	Achievement orientation	Working hard, hoping to accomplish the work tasks assigned by his/her superiors with flying colours, setting and achieving challenging personal and business targets by himself/herself, obtaining fulfilment in the process of success.
	Paying attention to details	Paying attention to detail, striving constantly for excellence, being careful and scrupulous, checking his/her work to make sure the required accuracy and integrality have been achieved

consciousness, service consciousness, consciousnesses and abilities of lifelong learning and innovation.

Other characteristics requirements are the personal characteristics assurance of high quality engineering and technical talent, which includes toughness, dedication and sense of responsibility, achievement orientation, and paying attention to details.

3 The Quality Assurance System for Master of Software Engineering

Base on the competency requirements summarized in Sect. 2, the quality assurance system for Master of software engineering is established. The quality assurance system includes educational goals setting, training scheme design, quality assurance of student source, quality assurance of faculty, assurance of supporting conditions, quality assurance of courses, quality assurance of industrial practice, quality assurance of dissertation, assurance of student development, quality evaluation and continual improvement, university-enterprise and international collaboration, and management system totally twelve sections. Among the sections, university-enterprise and international collaboration and management system run through the control process of the proposed educational quality assurance system, as shown in Fig. 1.

Accurate educational goals setting are the foundation of education quality assurance for Master of software engineering and must meet the requirements of the development of software industry.

The training scheme of Master of software engineering must fully support the achievement of the educational goals.

There is no doubt that the high quality of student source has a marked impact on the quality of graduated students. Before 2014, the national pilot schools of software had been granted to recruit students through independent tests and many quality problems in education of Master of software engineering were caused by the lax quality of admission. From 2014, all candidates have to attend the Graduate Candidate Test for Master of Engineering and from 2016, all candidates have to attend the National Graduate Unified Entrance Examination in the category of part-time education.

The quality of faculty focuses on the ability and experience of engineering, not only on the professional titles and academic degrees.

Assurance of supporting conditions means the number of recruited students cannot exceed the capability of supporting conditions in a university. From the viewpoint of education administration department, an upper limit of the number of students is to be set according to the educational supporting conditions in a university.

To ensure the quality of postgraduate courses for Master of software engineering, the courses contents should be determined with the participation of specialists

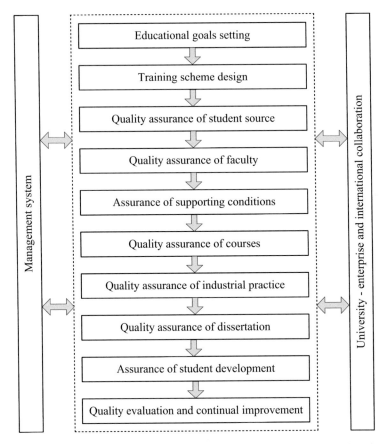

Fig. 1 Control process of the quality assurance system for Master of software engineering

from software enterprise and abroad to maintain the courses characteristics of engineering and internationalization. At HIT, a certain number of courses were taught by lecturers from the front of software industry and abroad.

Steady-going industrial practice bases are the foundation of high quality of industrial practice. Furthermore, a series of strict regulations should be set up scientifically to manage and evaluate the quality of student's industrial practice and the quality of the bases' running.

Besides the general requirements for dissertation of Master degree, the dissertation of Master of software engineering should be based on the actual engineering projects with clear application backgrounds. And the dissertation is to be completed under the direction both of the university supervisor and the enterprise supervisor.

Student development here means the training and development of student's process and consciousness abilities, and other characteristics in Table 1. The employment of students is also included in student development.

Quality evaluation should be done regularly for the aim of continual improvement. Continual improvement is not only a series of management documents, but also a set of mechanisms running well.

To ensure the characteristics of software engineering and internationalization, university-enterprise and international collaboration run through the entire control process of the proposed educational quality assurance system.

The management system in Fig. 1 means a series of regulations and mechanisms to ensure the high quality and well running of the other sections of the education quality assurance system.

4 Conclusions

With the boom of software industry, the education of Master of software engineering has also obtained a rapid development in China. At the same time, the quality problems in education of Master of software engineering have also caused the concern of the public and educational administrations. A suitable way to solve these problems is to establish a quality assurance system.

In this paper, the professional competency profile of the Master of software engineering have been investigated and summarized as the foundation of the quality assurance system. To achieve the goals of competency achievement, an education quality assurance system including twelve control sections is proposed. The preliminary running of the quality assurance system at the National Pilot School of Software at HIT has confirmed the validity of the proposed quality assurance system. Still, further and in-depth research, especially practical research needs to be done to improve the quality assurance system.

Acknowledgment This research was supported by the National Supervisory Committee for Education of Master of Engineering under Grant No. 2014-ZDn-07, Shandong Provincial Department of Education under Grant No. SDYY14003, and Harbin Institute of Technology under Grant No. JGYJ-201325 and WH2013009.

References

1. XU Xiaofei, LI Haifeng, WANG Ling, GUO Weihua. The "MSE + X" Programme in Software Engineering at HIT-NPSS. Computer Education, 2010(1):32–35.
2. Miao Yuan, Liu Xuning. Research of competency model of Master of software engineering. Academic Degrees and Graduate Education. 2009(3): 56–59.
3. Carol L. Hoover and Mary Shaw. The Carnegie Mellon University Master of Software Engineering Specialization Tracks. Proceedings of the Ninth Conference on Software Engineering Education, April 21–24, 1996: 100–118.
4. Pyster A, Turner R, Henry D. et al. Master's Degrees in Software Engineering: An Analysis of 28 University Programs. IEEE Software. 2009, 26(5): 94–101.

5. Sedelmaier Y. Landes D. Software engineering body of skills (SWEBOS). Proceedings of the IEEE Global Engineering Education Conference (EDUCON), April 3–5, 2014:395–401.
6. Liem I, Asnar Y, Akbar, S. Reshaping Software Engineering Education towards 2020 Engineers. Proceedings of the IEEE 27th Conference on Software Engineering Education and Training (CSEE&T), April 23–25, 2014: 171–174

Towards a Better Object-Oriented Software Development Education Using the DCI Software Architecture

Sofia Meacham, Keith Phalp, and Frank Grimm

1 Introduction

In most universities around Europe, including UK and Germany, many introductory-level courses in programming choose to start with teaching an object-oriented language such as Java or C++ as opposed to non-object oriented ones such as C, Pascal [1]. In the UK in particular, teaching coding with emphasis to object-orientation to children as young as five is part of the new computing curriculum with Scratch programming [2]. However, object-orientation as an aspect is not an easy theme neither grasp nor to teach especially at an introductory to programming level. Over the years, the authors have taught many university courses in object-oriented programming and have seen a lot of students having substantial difficulties in gaining an understanding for object-orientation. One of the authors taught first-year students how to program in Java. The majority of the students did not have prior experience with developing software and even those who had faced many difficulties finishing their assignments in time. Last term, the Python programming language was used instead of Java. The authors' expectation was that students new to programming would find it easier to start programming because Python requires much less "boilerplate" code to get started. While this expectation was actually met—it took students less time to start writing useful programs—their ability to write object-oriented software more complex than the simplistic introductory examples hasn't increased. While it would be easy to blame the teacher for being "unable" to teach even the basics of programming to students, this paper tries to give some more insight as to why the current approach to

S. Meacham • K. Phalp
Software Systems Research Centre, Bournemouth University, Dorset, UK

F. Grimm (✉)
Westsächsische Hochschule Zwickau – University of Applied Sciences, PSF 201037, Zwickau 08058, Germany
e-mail: fgr@fh-zwickau.de

© Springer International Publishing Switzerland 2016
S. Kassel, B. Wu (eds.), *Software Engineering Education Going Agile*, Progress in IS, DOI 10.1007/978-3-319-29166-6_16

113

teaching object-oriented programming is so hard for students to get acquainted with—and often results in badly written software. This paper also discusses an alternative approach to teaching object-oriented programming using the Data Context and Interaction (DCI) software architecture.

2   Class-Oriented Programming—Why Object-Oriented Programming Is Hard

When implementing object-oriented software, we teach our students to start with writing classes. A software system is designed building a (potentially large) number of classes. Later on, instances of these classes will be created to represent the objects of a software system. Following the object-oriented paradigm, classes encapsulate state and behaviour. Public methods define which messages an object of a class can receive, i.e., which behaviour it can execute. Private and protected methods might be used to implement some aspect of the public methods. Methods will change an object's state by changing the values of attributes.

In early stages of the development process, classes are neat and often follow the single responsibility principle [3, 4]. When the implementation grows, classes tend to become overloaded with complicated responsibilities. Despite studying and following common design patterns, students (and anyone else dealing with this code) lose the ability to maintain a clear mental model of the implementation. Trying to understand how one class works requires a lot of understanding of how other classes work. The class's raison d'etre is often not intentional and, thus, a program intentions are not obvious.

Here's a simple example of how simple programs can get complicated quite quickly: When designing and implementing object-oriented software, we tend to use nouns for the objects comprising software system because they help to reveal the intention of what these objects represent. For instance, when implementing software for electronically transferring money there might exist *Account* objects. A simple (simplistic even since a real-world implementation of an Account would use a ledger) implementation would consist of an *Account* class to store an amount of money associated with each *Account* object at runtime. Now, in order for the software be useful, an account holder should be able to deposit money to and withdraw money from an account:

1. User selects the source account from a list of available accounts.
2. User specifies amount to transfer.
3. System checks whether source account's balance is sufficient
4. If so, user is requested to select a different source account
5. User selects the destination account.
6. User initiates the transfer.
7. System tells user the source account's new balance.

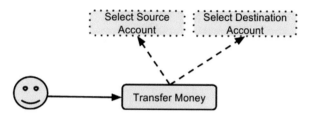

Fig. 1 Transfer Money use case

Two public methods increase funds and decrease funds are, therefore, added to the Account class. In addition, money should be transferred from one account to another. So, another method, transfer money, is added. The Account class is no longer just a representation of something that contains money. It now has the innate ability to deposit, withdraw, and transfer money as well. This seems perfectly acceptable. The Account class was created based on the responsibilities it has to fulfil. The object-oriented paradigm specifies that objects encapsulate data and behaviour. Any necessary data and behaviour for those objects is added to their class. Classes are used to specify the information and behaviour of objects created from them (cf., Fig. 1).

Following this approach, it is difficult to understand when a method will actually be used. In order to understand the program's behaviour a lot of classes have to be read and understood because each class implements many unrelated methods which are irrelevant for the program's actual behaviour. When trying to understand the meaning of an object, one has to understand all of its public methods even though many of them might be unrelated to the responsibilities the object is supposed to fulfil in a certain program context. All that is known is that these methods might be called at some point in the program's runtime—and might, thus, change an object's state.

For instance, in a money transfer specific scenario there are two *Account* objects, the source and the destination account. Since both objects are instances of the *Account* class, they can both transfer money to each other even though on the source account was intentioned to do so (cf. Fig. 2). This gets even worse when additional responsibilities are implemented for the Account class, e.g., to provide a list of all transactions or to close or reopen an account (cf. Fig. 3).

This is called *Restricted Object-Orientation* [5–7] because in order for programmers to understand how an object is used in a certain specific scenario, a lot of documentation and test code has to be taken into account. The programmer's mental map of a certain part of a program, therefore, will be large, much larger than the actual objects required to implement this specific scenario. Even worse, since documentation and test code has to be read while trying to understand a part of a program, many mental gaps between these different programming artifacts will occur and the programmer will be taken further away from the actual implementation. When new requirements are to be implemented, individual classes grow; new variable and public methods are added. This forces programmers to understand increasingly more about the implementation in its entirety to understand specific

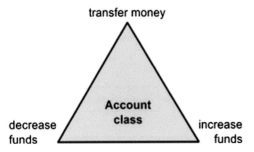

Fig. 2 Initial Account class containing only the implementation required for the Transfer Money use case

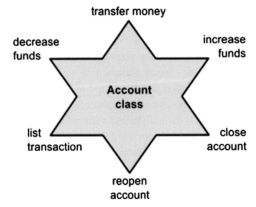

Fig. 3 Account class containing the implementations of several use cases

scenarios. This makes programs hard to read since the goal of readable programs can only be achieved by manually restricting the number of public methods an object's class implements [8]. Since an object's behaviour has to be understood from within its corresponding class, it is difficult to build a concrete understanding of how and when objects interact. "It is unclear what objects are present and of what methods they require at any given point. A programmer can understand the program behavior only in general terms." [9]

3 DCI: Object-Oriented Programming with Objects and Roles

Therefore, there is a need for a new approach to teach object-orientation that will reduce the amount of information that you need to take into account in order to understand an object's behaviour.

DCI is an object-oriented software architecture and it stands for Data, Context, Interaction. It enables programmers to write software that can be better understood in terms of object collaboration and runtime execution. "The mental model is reified in readable code" as the DCI inventors, Trygve Reenskaug and James Coplien state [10]. It is a software architecture which adds algorithms for object collaboration. These algorithms are implemented in DCI Contexts. Together with Interactions, Contexts specify what the software system does. The third parts of DCI is Data, it defines what the system is. This separation divides a program's implementation into two projections, the Data projection describing the system state and the Context projection describing its behaviour. Separating implementations into these two views results in a clear separation between the rapidly changing parts of the system, i.e., the behaviour—what the system does—and the slowly changing part, i.e., the domain or data model—what the system is. The Data projection corresponds to classic class-oriented programming. Interactions are part of the Context projection and are the key innovation of DCI added to object-oriented programming. They implement a functional decomposition of a Context's functionality. This function-ality is implemented by objects interacting with each other. These objects are referred to by the roles they play in an Interaction. The role an object plays is independent from the object's type, i.e., its class. For an object to play a certain role, it is only relevant that it can execute the behaviour this roles is expected to provide. "Roughly speaking, the class is on the inside and the role is on the outside of the Context projection." [9] The same object will play different roles in different Contexts. Its behaviour is, therefore, dynamically extended during the program's runtime as so-called role methods are dynamically added to the object in order to fulfil its different roles in different Contexts.

4 DCI Details and Example

In Fig. 4 there is a version of the money transfer example discussed above implemented in a DCI-conforming way. The domain model, i.e., the Data projec-tion part of DCI, consists of the Account class. This class defines a balance attribute and two public methods, increase funds and decrease funds. This is all behaviour and state required to implement the 'what the system is' aspect.

The 'what the system does' aspect consists of the DCI Contexts projection defining its behaviour. Contexts correspond to the use cases a software system implements. In the example discussed here, the—arguably simplified—use case is transferring money from a source account to a destination account. Each Context represents exactly one use case making it easy for the developer to see the business logic directly as an algorithm in the source code. This allows to close the gap between the end user's mental model of a use case and the developer's understanding of it. Bridging this gap is often hard to do since mental models are difficult to communicate and prone to misunderstanding [11]. Failing to under-stand the business logic and the end user's mental model of it will lead to

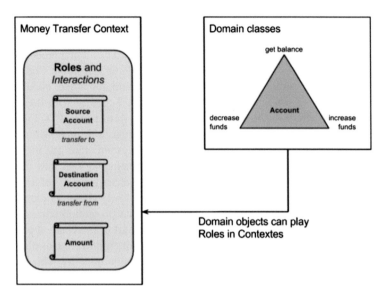

Fig. 4 DCI implementation of the Transfer Money use case [10]

program errors. In addition, the programmer's understanding of a business logic might be incomplete during the initial implementation—as might the end user's understanding. The resulting implementation will, therefore, be incomplete and buggy. When the logic get more and more discovered and understood by all involved parties, the implementation inevitable will have to change. The DCI approach allows to separate the business logic from the domain models. Therefore, the implementation, i.e., the software architecture, supports change. Supporting one of the most important goals of agile software development, customer collaboration and responding to change, end users and developers can discuss about, incrementally develop, and validate the business logic a program implements by reasoning about the implementation. Following the DCI approach, source code can be structured in a way that allows to better communicate how the components of a program—i.e., it variables, methods, and classes—fit together.

Separating Contexts from each other allows to think of a program in terms of its use cases; each Context implements a different one. A Context's algorithm— implementing the use case—is based on the roles defined for this Context. Data objects, i.e., domain objects, are assigned roles when a Context is initialised. The same domain object can play different roles in different Contexts. In DCI, it is also possible to create recursive Contexts in order to further refine an implementation. A Context, then, plays a role in another Context.

In DCI, the (domain) class hierarchy is separated from the (hierarchy of) Contexts. All system behaviour is implemented as Contexts. This orthogonal approach allows to separate the fast changing parts of a program, i.e., use cases implemented by Contexts, to be separated from the stable parts, i.e., the classes representing the domain model.

When domain objects play a certain role in a Context, they get assigned so-called Role Methods. This means that—when a Context is initialised—objects are temporarily extended with Role Methods required to fulfil a certain role in a Context. A context's algorithm is then implemented based on the Role Methods. A great advantage of this functional decomposition is that programmers can reason about system behaviour without having to understand the classes of the role-playing objects—programmers can focus on the Role Methods as they fully define the behaviour of a role-playing object in a Context.

For the money transfer use case this means that a Money Transfer Context will implement this use case. There are three roles that are required, the source and destination account, and the amount of money to be transferred. The source account role can be played by any domain object that provides behaviour to get the account's balance and decrease its funds; for instance, an Account object can take on the role of a source account. The destination account role can be played by any object that provides behaviour to increase funds. So, an Account object can play this role, too:

The role of the amount of money to be transferred is simply played by a number (potentially attributed with a currency). The Context defines a 'transfer money' role method which gets the source and destination Account instances and the amount of money to be transferred, assigns them the source account role to the Account instance supposed to act as the source account and, respectively, the destination account role. By assigning these roles, each Account object gets temporarily assigned the Role Methods of the respective role. The source account role defines a 'transfer to' Role Method and the target account role a 'transfer from' Role Method.

The algorithm implementing the money transfer then uses these Role Methods to realise the business logic. The 'transfer to' Role Method first checks if the source account has sufficient funds. If so, the source accounts funds are decreased by the amount of money to be transferred, then, the destination account's 'transfer to' Role Method is called which increases the funds by the amount of money to be transferred.

A great advantage of Contexts, therefore, is that they allow implementing business logic in a sequential manner in a singular spot of the source code—something which is often impossible with purely class-based approaches to object-oriented programming. So programmers can reason about a use case's implementation reading the algorithm in the Context from top to bottom without the need to read additional source code elsewhere. Here is the money transfer example algorithm:

1. 'Money transfer' Context projection:

   (a) roles: source account; destination account; amount of money to be transferred
   (b) Role Method: 'transfer'

- assigns roles to domain objects and
- calls 'transfer to' Role Method on 'source account' role

(c) Interaction/algorithm (business logic):

- Role Method 'transfer to' on 'source account' role:

  - Check 'source account's (self instance) balance against amount of money to be transferred

    If insufficient funds, raise an exception

  - Call 'decrease money' method on 'source account' role (self instance)
  - Call 'transfer from' Role Method on 'destination account' role

- Role Method 'transfer from' on 'destination account' role

  - trigger 'increase funds' on 'destination account' role (self instance)

5 Combining DCI and MVC and Conclusions

DCI fits well with the Model-View-Controller (MVC) paradigm which is taught as part of many university object-oriented programming courses. DCI and MVC complement each other. MVC is used to present the domain model to end users in a way that conforms to their understanding of these elements, i.e., their mental model. MVC connects the user interface elements end users utilise to interact with a computer to the use cases realised by DCI Contexts. The combination of MVC and DCI can, therefore, support students new to object-oriented programming to better structure their source code since both paradigms focus on capturing the end user's understanding/mental model of a real-world process in source code. End users primarily reason about real-world objects by the roles these object play in the end user's mental model—the actual type of the objects is mostly irrelevant for an end user. DCI's roles, therefore, help to capture the end user's mental model in source code and bring it close programmer's mental model. Thus, DCI and MVC support to create a shared mental model between the real world and the programming world. This will help students new to programming to transform use cases to readable software they can reason about.

References

1. Kölling, Michael; Koch, Bett; Rosenberg, John. Requirements for a First Year Object-Oriented Teaching Language. SIGCSE Bulletin, Vol. 27, No. 1, Mar. 1995, pp. 173–177
2. Smith, Neil; Sutcliffe, Clare and Sandvik, Linda (2014). Code Club: bringing programming to UK primary schools through Scratch. In: 45th ACM Technical Symposium on Computer Science Education (SIGCSE14), 5–8 March 2014, Atlanta, GA, ACM.

3. DeMarco, Tom. (1979). Structured Analysis and System Specification. Prentice Hall. ISBN 0-13-854380-1.
4. Martin, Robert C. (2002). Agile Software Development, Principles, Patterns, and Practices. Prentice Hall. ISBN 0-13-597444-5.
5. Reenskaug, Trygve: DCI Execution Model; April 2013; Online resource: http://fulloo.info/Documents/DCIExecutionModel-2.1.pdf [accessed 15 February 2015]
6. Reenskaug, Trygve; Wold, Per; Lehne, Odd Arild: Working With Objects: The OOram Software Engineering Method. Manning/Prentice Hall 1996; ISBN 0-13-452930-8
7. Coplien, James O.; Bjørnvig, Gertrude: Lean Architecture for Agile Software Development. Wiley, Chichester, UK, 2010; ISBN 978-0-470-68420-7
8. Reenskaug, Trygve: The Case for Readable Code. Klein: Computer Software Engineering Research; Expert Commentary; pp. 3–8; Nova Science Publishers, New York, 2007; ISBN: 978-1-60021-774-6
9. Coplien, James O.; Reenskaug, Trygve: The data, context and interaction paradigm. In Gary T. Leavens (Ed.): Conference on Systems, Programming, and Applications: Software for Humanity, SPLASH '12, Tucson, AZ, USA, October 21–25, 2012. ACM 2012, ISBN 978-1-4503-1563-0, pp. 227–228
10. Reenskaug, Trygve; Coplien, James O.: Working with objects—in computer and mind. 26 January 2014. Online resource: http://fulloo.info/Documents/CommSenseCurrentDraft.pdf [accessed 15 February 2015]
11. Norman, Don: Some Observations on Mental Models. In Human-computer Interaction. Baecker, R. M. and Buxton, W. A. S., editors. Morgan Kaufmann Publishers Inc 1987.

Principled Flipped Learning Paradigm for Laboratory Courses in Software Engineering

Tonghua Su, Shengchun Deng, Xiaofei Xu, Dong Li, and Zhiying Tu

1 Introduction

Software engineering is an applied discipline to solve the challenging in the rapid changing information technology world. In recent years, universities in China have faced great issues for their failure to adequately educate students [1]. Even some students failed to program for simple software requirements after four-year long undergraduate education programme. Certainly, the lecture-based or instructor-centered instructional approach can hardly engage students and develop their critical thinking and problem-solving skills. Ongoing concerns about the quality of future software engineers have prompted numerous calls for pedagogical reform [2].

One of the seismic shifts is in the form of flipped learning. In the traditional classroom, professors spend the majority of their time delivering lectures while the students spend their most class time taking notes. Professors have little time to help them connect the analytical dots [3]. Different from the traditional classroom, the flipped learning (also known as the flipped, reverse, inverse, or backwards classroom), instructors prerecord lectures and post them online for students to watch on their own so that class time can be dedicated to student-centered learning activities, like problem-based learning and inquiry-oriented strategies [4]. Therefore, the two main phases of instruction are "flipped" or reversed. Instead of students listening to a lecture on, say, parallel programming in class and then going home to work on a set of assigned problems. They read material and view videos on parallel programming before coming to class and then engage in class in active learning using case studies, labs, games, simulations, or experiments.

T. Su (✉) • S. Deng • X. Xu • D. Li • Z. Tu
School of Software, Harbin Institute of Technology, Harbin, China
e-mail: thsu@hit.edu.cn

© Springer International Publishing Switzerland 2016
S. Kassel, B. Wu (eds.), *Software Engineering Education Going Agile*, Progress in IS, DOI 10.1007/978-3-319-29166-6_17

Recent studies show that flipped learning poses great advantages than traditional curricula. Kathleen Fulton has a thorough discussion on those advantages [5]. Based on their discussion, we can summarize the following points: (1) students move at their own pace; (2) doing "homework" in class gives teachers better insight into student difficulties and learning styles; (3) classroom time can be used more effectively and creatively; (4) teachers using the method report seeing increased levels of student achievement, interest, and engagement. A survey on more than 200 teachers provides additional reasons for adopting flipped classroom [6]: (5) is more time to spend with students on authentic research; (6) students get more time working with scientific equipment that is only available in the classroom; (7) students who miss class for debate/sports/etc. can watch the lectures while on the road; (8) the method promotes critical thinking inside and outside of the classroom; (9) students are more actively involved in the learning process.

In light of the success practices, we present a principled flipped learning paradigm for laboratory course in software engineering. It integrates three models each of which assures the curricula from different perspective. The goal-assessment model measures and controls the quality of the ongoing course. If there is any imperfectness detected by the evolutionary model, the process model will be renewed. All of them are coupled in a systemic way to foster active learning and engagement.

The next section proposes the principled paradigm that aims for a active laboratory learning course. In Sect. 3, a flipped learning practice is conducted following the paradigm. Finally, brief conclusions are given.

2 Paradigm

Laboratory courses in software engineering are more problem solving oriented than regular ones, thus flipped learning seems to be an effective teaching approach. We propose a principled paradigm to facilitate such curriculum. The paradigm is composed of three models that run together as shown in Fig. 1: the goal-assessment model, the process model, and the course evolutionary model.

The goal-assessment model breakdown the general course objective into manageable subgoals as shown in Fig. 2, following a divide-then-conquer strategy. A course may include several units, so the course objective can be transformed as a series of unit-level subgoals. Here the word "unit" includes but not limited to labs, projects.

The process model controls the learning process and attempts to realize the course objective. The process model follows a spiral model that is a popular rational model in traditional software development process [7], as illustrated in Fig. 3. Each cycle realize one subgoal of the course and the next cycle moves to higher subgoal. However, during its runtime, it is organized as several phases until reaching the end of the course: offline content preparation phase, lab phase, project phase and finally the summary phase. These phases follow a simple Waterfall look-alike model [8].

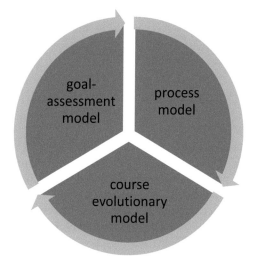

Fig. 1 The structure of paradigm

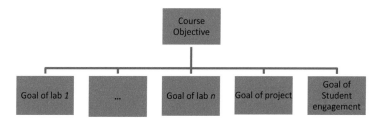

Fig. 2 Goal-assessment Model

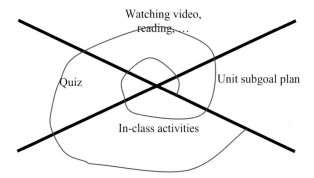

Fig. 3 Spiral Process Model

Finally, the course evolutionary model connects the aforementioned two models together. If there is any unsatisfied subgoal, then the course process model will be renewed in the next cycle or next semester. Not only the lab subgoal and project subgoal is evaluated, but the student response and engagement status are considered. Such error-correcting style is similar to the perceptron algorithm [9] in machine learning field.

3   Practice

We applied our proposed flipped learning paradigm to an innovative laboratory course entitled "High Performance GPU Programming". This course is to teach students the parallel programming skills underlying data-intensive computation. Thus, it is a project-intensive course with significant coding, writing, and presenting. We had selected about 30 students from diverse disciplines in year 2013 and 2014 respectively. In year 2013, we employed a traditional approach: gave lectures in class and left most labs and project out-class. As for 2014, we offloaded the in-class lectures to self-paced online videos and class time is dedicated to engaging students in active learning activities, like discuss open questions, sharing idea, doing labs, implementing project in group. During the class time, students read and learn information on their own, but instructors act as coaches and mentors to stimulate and challenge their thinking, guide them in solving problems, and encourage their learning and application of the material.

In our flipped learning version, the course objective is partitioned into four lab subgoals and one project subgoal. Using this philosophy, we can manage to reach the course objective in a step-by-step, easy-to-complex way. The process model is utilized to guiding the whole course runtime. The first lab requests that students write their own vector-addition kernel and deal with the errors. The second lab is about the analysis of the GPU warp scheduling and then writing a Euclidean distance-computing kernel. The third lab is to solve the Monte Carlo simulation and Finite difference equations. Moreover, the last lab is to implement an efficient parallel reduction algorithm. Through those experiences learned from those four labs, the students develop their problem-solving ability. Therefore, we can ask them to conquer the real-world problems such as signal visualization, fast convolutional neural network, clustering data-intensive computation. The course will be redesigned in the next semester considering the collected erroneous samples. This evolutionary model can improve the course continuously.

To partially evaluate the effectiveness of our flipped learning. We collected the student's resultant performance of year 2013 and 2014, and plotted in Figs. 4 and 5, respectively. Seen from figures, unlike year 2013, majority of the students get good grades and smaller students fail to pass the laboratory course in year 2014.

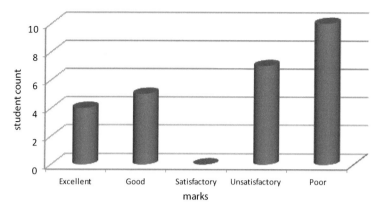

Fig. 4 Student Performance in Year 2013

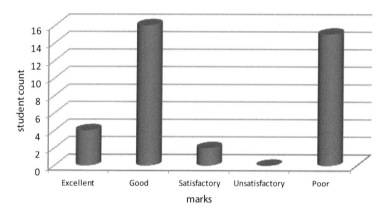

Fig. 5 Student Performance in Year 2014

4 Conclusions

This paper presents a principled flipped learning paradigm for laboratory course in software engineering. The paradigm consists of three instruction models and they can work together to enhance the engagement of students. The effectiveness of the proposed paradigm is evaluated in our practice.

References

1. Xiaolin Xu, Hong Lu, The Exploration and Practice of Blending eaching Model on the Course of Program Design Basis, IT Education, 2007(20):15–17(in Chinese).

2. Mingxing Zeng, Qingping Zhou, et al., Research on Flipped Classroom Models for Software Development Courses. Research and Exploration in Laboratory, 2014,33(2):203–209 (in Chinese).
3. William R. Slomanson, Blended Learning: A Flipped Classroom Experiment, Journal of Legal Education, 2014,64(1):93–102.
4. Jacqueline E. McLaughlin, Mary T. Roth, et al., Flipped Classroom: A Course Redesign to Foster Learning and Engagement in a Health Professions School,2014,89(2):236–242.
5. Kathleen Fulton, Upside Down and Inside Out: Flip Your Classroom to Improve Student Learning. Learning & Leading with Technology, 2012,39(8):12–17.
6. Clyde Freeman Herreid, Nancy A. Schiller, Case Studies and the Flipped Classroom, Journal of College Science Teaching:2013,42(5):62–66.
7. Boehm B. A Spiral Model of Software Development and Enhancement. IEEE Computer, 1988,21(5):61–72.
8. Winston W. Royce, Managing the Development of Large Software Systems, Proc. IEEE WESTCON, 1970.
9. Rosenblatt F, The Perceptron: A Probabilistic Model for Information Storage and Organization in the Brain, Psychological Review, 1958,65 (6):386–408.

Printed in the United States
By Bookmasters